COOLESCAPES

Boutique Homes
Handpicked Vacation Rentals

edited by
Heinz Legler, Veronique Lievre
Martin Nicholas Kunz

avedition

TABLE OF CONTENTS

After downloading the "Cool Escapes Boutique Homes" app on your smartphone, go to the menu bar and select INTERACTIVE. Then, hold your smartphone camera to the intro page and any other page in the book showing Boutique Homes. You will directly be connected to the property page in the app to watch videos, open extended image galleries, start soundtracks or visit related websites. Welcome to our interactive coffee table book, connecting fine print with the digital world and elevating our reading experience to a new level.

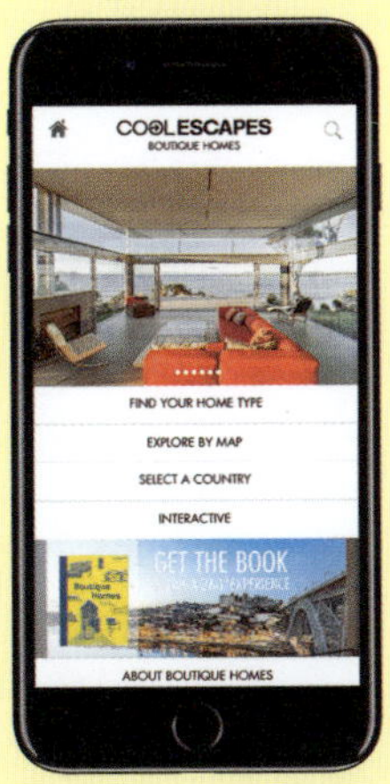

WE ARE OBVIOUSLY LIKE-MINDED

In 2008, we wrote an article for our website been-seen.com about the frustration we used to feel looking for vacation rentals that lived up to our aesthetics and style. We felt as if going on vacation was always coupled with accepting accommodations which were not up to our standards.

At that time, finding a private, cool place to stay was like searching for a needle in a haystack. The search was pretty time-consuming and mostly frustrating. There was not much out there—yet! But what a development there has been over the last decade.

When we were children, the idea of renting out our homes to strangers was unthinkable. Letting strangers sleep in your bed, use your kitchen and take a shower in your bathroom was not an option. But over the last few years, the vacation rental business has changed radically, thanks to the sharing economy, coupled with the internet.

We believe people started sharing their homes for two main reasons. First of all, the sharing economy offered a new stream of extra income, and many jumped on that. Secondly, the idea of sharing what you have to offer was appealing. It was fun and satisfying to let others stay in your personal space, to display how you live, what you like, and how creative you have been in designing your home.

Meanwhile, travelers started to look for different kinds of experiences when traveling or on vacation. The slogan "live like a local" was born, and a match in heaven was made. Hosts opened their doors to let travelers experience their personal homes and neighborhoods. The combination of both created a new breed of entrepreneurs: the micro-hoteliers.

FROM BOUTIQUE HOTELS TO BOUTIQUE HOMES

Over time, a lot of these new, private, personally-styled homes became available for sharing. Some of the new micro-hoteliers went as far as replicating qualities that, up to that point, had been reserved for hotels. Their photographs showed details of how they nicely arranged the towels, a picture of a fruit plate, the assortment of toiletries... What started out as a possible additional income source had turned for many into a fun decorating and interior-design project.

People started remodeling barns, train stations, garages and garden sheds for the sole purpose of sharing them as short-term rentals. Architects designed prefab homes to be utilized as vacation rentals. Others specialized, zooming in on some new terms like "holiday architecture" or "living architecture".

Eight years on, the landscape has changed drastically, and today we are busier than ever, keeping up with all the new, cool, hip and stylish spaces that are popping up all over the world.

We have been in it from the beginning, and this book documents the evolution and highlights of this amazing development. It showcases the best of this new private and personal hospitality concept and approach.

GOING FORWARD

With big players like Expedia, Hotels.com and even (of late) Google adding vacation rentals to the line of products they offer, vacation rentals have grown up and have now become a widely-accepted form of travel accommodation.

At the same time, opening up this option to a mass market doesn't mean individual, personal, intimate homes will become obsolete. The opposite. We think a carefully curated selection of modern vacation homes is needed more than ever.

At Boutique Homes, we have created a community of travelers and homeowners who do not want to be treated as anonymous consumers or as just another product to be added to an inventory. Our travelers share common ground, our property owners love what they do, and we love what we do. We are obviously like-minded.

We still consider ourselves gem hunters, looking for those special places that design lovers hope to discover for their next trip. We find them, and those special gems find us, and their owners are happy that there is a website where their vacation home feels at home.

Curation has always had its place, providing experience and knowledge when people are overwhelmed and looking for guides, instead of sifting through a vast number of options. We see our future right there. Boutique Homes is the chic nomad's guide.

Veronique Lievre and Heinz Legler completed Verana—the handmade hotel (verana.com) in 2000 and built Far Meadow, a mountain camp (farmeadow.com) near Yosemite, in 2005. They went on to create Boutique Homes in 2008 and have curated over 1,200 handpicked modern vacation homes and very small hotels on their site (boutique-homes.com), for a community of like-minded design lovers. When they aren't in their Topanga, California home and Boutique Homes office, they can be found visiting properties curated on their site—or at their favorite hideaways in Big Sur and Corsica.

Nancy Bachmann is a conscious living advocate and publisher / producer. A native of Germany, she lives in Los Angeles and is moved to spread positivity around the globe. She's a partner in Smart Travelling (smart-travelling.net), an award winning print & online travel guide and author of "A Perfect Week / Weekend..." with over 60 books published. She is also the Co-Founder of Los Angeles Cold Press lacoldpress.com, a cold press juice company, motivated to bring the healthy Californian lifestyle to Berlin and beyond.

photo by Eva Napp

THE LUXURY OF SPACE AND TIME

At first glance, emotion and luxury appear incongruous. The familiar "must have" feeling associated with both luxury products and experiences has always fallen terribly short of furnishing its participant with a truly individual and unique emotive experience.

Further complicated by the current digital age, the whirlwind of everyday life both heightens our hunger for deeper personal connection while making the conditions to satisfy those connections we crave more elusive. The language of luxury has evolved to speak to our desire for authentic meaningful exchanges, whether that be with product or environment.

The following houses rise to the challenge of this new luxury. Inspired by their surrounding nature, these homes effortlessly marry the unique and personal with the elevated luxury of beauty and superior design. Providing a wide variety of aesthetics, these places reflect traditional elements native to the cultural backdrop of their locations while incorporating the amenities of modern living. The ancient and the modern coexist seamlessly.

Allowing the stories of these places to inspire us to reimagine dreamlike ways of living and recalling an appreciation for the slowness of an analog life. Thoughtful and authentic design, connecting with nature, the history and the spirit of a place—all of this becomes a part of a new definition of luxury.

These unique and intimate homes welcome us to truly feel our senses and to experience their design and intention in a way that will allow us to reach distant parts of our emotions, to journey into our own hearts.

They are the vehicle through which we can reawaken our instinctive connection to the land. Acting as a sanctuary, these homes enable guests to engage in personal rejuvenation and reflection by tapping into the meaningful exchange between self and space. This is how perspectives are broadening and new horizons are forged. These are the elements of a truly unique and transcendent experience. This is modern luxury embodied.

— Nancy Bachmann

AT THE WATER'S EDGE

Léonard Lièvre lives on the French coast of Normandy in a home he designed himself. He is a contributing editor for Boutique Homes and he's passionate about travel and art. Léonard is a former student in art history of the Ecole du Louvre, in Paris. He travels mainly in Europe and especially in the Mediterranean region, where he visits owners of beautiful houses to discuss their creative process and the story behind the scenes. He also collaborates as a journalist for several French newspapers including the well known Le Canard Enchaîné.

photo by Antoine Lièvre

Beneath my windows, the ocean waves come crashing down at the foot of the dunes and cliffs in the distance. From where I stand, just a few feet from the edge of the sea, I almost feel as if I can see the Earth's curve on the horizon. And suddenly, it is no longer the Earth that I see, but the entire Universe. The water, the air, the void and the planets scroll past my eyes like a cosmic, vertiginous vision. I like the idea that if I were to land one day on the opposite side of this spectrum, lost in space or stranded on some far away comet, I could make out the minuscule point which is my house. Almost at first glance, just by staring at the Earth and following the continent's line, as if I were caressing its coast.

I also like the idea that beneath the sea facing me, under this mass that shimmers and shivers and at times beats like a huge heart, there are creatures, thousands of them, almost as many as there are stars in the sky, that live together, love one another and fight each other. It is as if these houses dotted along the coastline are both driven towards the abyss, and rising up to the celestial arch.

These houses are unlike any of the others, positioned on the cusp of two worlds, turning their backs to trees, to men and their tormented lives. I believe that if they could, these houses would choose to escape the noise and fuss of a land which they must feel is too narrow and too conventional.

I find myself meandering barefoot through the rooms of my divine companion, walking from hall to terrace, then across to the garden and its exotic plants, guided by the sounds of roaring waves and singing birds. I glide among the smells from the sea spray and the heath, in a sort of sensual, pagan meditation. At dusk, as I stand in the wind taking in my surroundings, I almost feel that my home is like a loved one, looking over and protecting me.

— Léonard Lièvre

SCHOOLHOUSE

Nova Scotia, Canada

SCHOOLHOUSE

WHAT WE LIKE

This gorgeous little schoolhouse is not only a cool throwback to another time and place, but it's located, according to its owners, at "the end of the Earth". Which makes for a really unique experience. By that, they mean that it sits between mountains and the Atlantic Ocean, on a remote peninsula in Nova Scotia.

designed by Brian MacKay-Lyons
photos by William Green

School House on the Peninsula

An elegant and simple design but with so much character, this 19th-century schoolhouse retains many original features and lets its history speak for itself. Uncluttered, with strong lines and ample space for up to five guests, it boasts beautiful views of the Atlantic coastline and an extraordinary remote location. Over the years, local architect and owner Brian MacKay-Lyons has been creating new properties on this former farm, and this one was actually brought here from the community where he was born and raised. Dating back to 1830, it has clapboard walls, a cedar-shingled roof, pine floor boards, and original windows from the period. On the main level, the "great room" still feels like the original schoolhouse, and its open-plan layout has kitchen, dining and living areas, with a freestanding wood stove and restored wooden benches.

The second floor has two bedrooms—a master with a modern wood stove, and a bunk room sleeping area. The house has its own six-person hot tub on a deck overlooking the ocean, and a private barbecue. The complex is made up of several structures, all of which are of great architectural interest and all of which can be rented, making it perfect for large groups or events. The property aims to be sustainable, with such features as free-roaming sheep, an organic vegetable garden and trout ponds, as well as solar energy.

This is a property for the adventurous, well off the beaten track—but perfect for relaxing getaways and creative endeavors. "If you're looking for Motel 6, you don't come here," say the owners. "If you're looking for nature and a physical relationship to nature —kayaking, swimming, surfing, fishing— you come here. If you want to be alone and write a book, you can do that as well."

HOLBOX ISLAND BUNGALOW

Holbox, Mexico

HOLBOX ISLAND BUNGALOW

A Yucatan Island Hideaway

Just a short walk from the beach and the center of Holbox village, this beach house is nestled among the coconut groves in a peaceful and private hideaway, yet near to all that the island has to offer. Built in a fusion of Mayan and Moroccan-inspired style, the three-story house is a pristine and dreamy space with cool whitewashed walls and a rustic-luxe design aesthetic. Guests have access to the second level loft space and living area with a shady palm fringed balcony for reading and siestas as well as a cozy double bedroom adjacent to a well equipped kitchen and bathroom. Designed with an eye for detail, the carefully selected furnishings, art and decor create a serene balance of earthiness and style.

The spiral staircase winds up to the rooftop terrace and sun deck with a yoga shala and bungalow lounge. It's the ideal spot for lazy afternoons in the hammock, sunset cocktails, and balmy stargazing by night.

interiors by Marco Badalian
photos by Marco Badalian Photography

WHAT WE LIKE

A bohemian hideaway that artfully blends the style and influences of the Yucatan, Morocco and the southwest, this beach house lies along the shores of tiny Holbox Island, where you can escape to an undiscovered corner of the Yucatan. Pristine and relaxing, we love the rooftop terrace and lounge from where you can catch the island sunsets and the night time stars.

PALAPA BEACH HOUSE

Sayulita, Mexico

PALAPA BEACH HOUSE

WHAT WE LIKE

With splashes of bold color, vivid fabrics, stained glass and an entrance hall that feels a little like a hidden temple, this beach house is a unique and rustic retreat on the Mexican Riviera.

designed by Brian Hodges & Sophie Hodges
photos by Brian Hodges

Sayulita by the Sea

This two-building Mexican beach house is surrounded by lush vegetation and has a lovely earthy bohemian feel.

Bright, airy and colorful, the property sits above the shore overlooking the charming fishing and surfing town of Sayulita. The main house is a whitewashed stone structure with a tiled roof, tiled floors and wooden floors, beams and decking. The secondary structure is a breezy two-story palapa. Two of the three independent bedrooms are in the main house—the master bedroom, with its lavish views of the ocean, and an additional guest room for two. The third bedroom is in the detached palapa accessed by a ladder. Offering plenty of space for up to 10 guests, the property has a wonderfully relaxed—slightly wild—atmosphere and plenty of indoor/outdoor living space, including expansive decking at the tree tops. The large gardens, and great outdoor living areas are draped in lush vegetation with lovely views of the town and coastline.

NESKOWIN BEACH HOUSE

Neskowin, Oregon

NESKOWIN BEACH HOUSE

Spotlight on the Oregon Coast

Designed by Portland-based architect Cornell Anderson, this modern home sits in splendid seclusion along Oregon's rugged central coast, with panoramic views that stretch for miles. Placed above a coastal inlet of protected wetlands with vast expanses of pristine shoreline, the house was designed to complement the landscape. Constructed of clean sculptural lines and an abundance of natural wood, concrete and glass, the house features meticulously crafted details and finishes.

The open-plan great room soars to double heights with floor to ceiling windows and a large retractable door that opens out to the deck overlooking the marshlands and the sea providing a continuous flow between the fireside living spaces and the eat-in chef's kitchen and dining area. Dominated by the glass walls that focus outward, the main floor ascends to an open mezzanine office space above the two double bedrooms below. The en-suite master features its own cozy wood stove and a luxurious Japanese soaking tub and both have private ocean views and an abundance of natural light.

The deck is perfect for entertaining and dining al fresco with a fireplace and comfy spots to lounge overlooking the shore with paths from the house leading down to the beach.

This house is the ideal retreat that showcases the juxtaposition of great modern design and the dramatic beauty of the land and sea.

designed by Cornell Anderson, Fieldwork Design Portland
photos by Gemma and Andrew Ingalls

WHAT WE LIKE

The spectacular Oregon coastline is one of our favorites, and this house's strong linear lines and retractable walls of glass captures its stunning natural beauty to great effect. With soaring open interiors, sleek contemporary style and innovative indoor outdoor layout, the house is thoughtfully designed with stylish simplicity and the emphasis of nature in mind.

COASTAL GLASS HOUSE

Tasmania, Australia

COASTAL GLASS HOUSE

Revealing Design

A remarkable achievement in glass, light and space, this one-of-a-kind home sits on a bluff overlooking Great Oyster Bay with unobstructed "forever" views. Surrounded by ocean and national parkland, this is a once-in-a-lifetime spot that takes full advantage of the secluded location while creating both a contrasting and harmonious residence.

The bold, spare, metal post and beam construction paired with the endless walls of glass is an exhilarating living experience. The carefully selected decor and modern art barely interrupt the space but are just as bold with contemporary silhouettes and spirited use of color and animal prints. The fireplace and heated stone floors bring warmth and relaxation while the outdoor decks and lounge areas take you away with the endless views.

Serene and modern, the home features three bedrooms all with handmade Stuart Houghton Tasmanian oak beds and floor-to-ceiling windows. One of the three baths features a unique, deep Huon pine tub, all with an abundance of natural light.

WHAT WE LIKE

It was hard for us to tell where the landscape ended and the house began. The majestic location and breathtaking views, the private beach and innovative design creates an inspired and dramatic architectural composition.

designed by Craig Rosevears
photos by Jonathan Wherrett

PIGEON BAY

Canterbury, New Zealand

Drama and Seclusion

This award-winning home, on the Banks Peninsula in the dramatic volcanic landscape of New Zealand's South Island, is nestled into a rocky escarpment in a sheltered cove with breathtaking views of the coast. Conceived and designed by Auckland-based architect Andrew Patterson, the home is constructed largely from locally quarried stone, steel and glass with a poured concrete floor and an earth turfed roof. Accessible only by helicopter or 4-wheel-drive vehicle, the location is remote and secluded and was designed as a romantic hideaway for two. The horizontal silhouette is seamlessly integrated into the land in perfect relationship to the natural environment and consists of just three irregularly shaped rooms. The open-plan layout includes the main living area with a split level separation between the bedroom area with walls of glass overlooking the coast. The sleek modern kitchen is off to the side and the cave-like bathroom at the back features a deep freestanding tub with a view out to the terrace.

The interlocking geometric design corresponds to both views of the bay and distant views out to Rocky Spire appearing as if you are floating on the open sea. The dramatic rock, concrete and sleek modernism are softened by a selection of soft, neutral textiles and animal hides and contemporary furnishings including a suspended Eero Aarnio Bubble chair for taking in the views and lounging in front of the fire. The outdoor lounge is positioned for maximum effect with a fireplace and spa pool to complete the romantic tone.

Winner of the 2014 Urbis Award for Best House and Home of the Year finalist from HOME Magazine, the house is also eco-friendly and incorporated an extensive reforestation and re-vegetation effort.

Set in striking harmony within its awe-inspiring landscape, this award-winning home has perfected its place within the environment evoking a strong sense of belonging. Exquisitely composed with natural materials and innovative modern design principles, we love the feeling of calm sophistication and timeless beauty.

designed by Andrew Patterson
photos by Simon Devitt, courtesy of Patterson Associates

SCRUBBY BAY

Annandale, New Zealand

SCRUBBY BAY

Composition and Landscape in Harmony

Placed within the dramatic volcanic landscape along the Bank's Peninsula of New Zealand's South Island, this award-winning home is designed as the centerpiece of a remote and wild cove with breathtaking views of the ocean and mountains. Conceived and designed by Auckland-based architect Andrew Patterson, the home was commissioned by an expatriate New Zealander as a base for farm and coastal activities and is part of a large homestead originally settled in the late 19th century. Accessible only by helicopter or 4-wheel-drive vehicle, the property was designed as a rural farm retreat for up to 14 guests.

Shortlisted for the World Building of the Year, the house is constructed largely from locally sourced macrocarpa wood, quarried stone and steel, its horizontal silhouette seamlessly integrated into the land in perfect relationship to the natural environment. The open-plan layout includes the towering great room with a large stone fireplace and walls of glass overlooking the shore, with both seaward and leeward exterior environments. The sleek modern kitchen is off to the side and is perfect for entertaining with a dining area opposite the fireplace that seats 14. There are three oceanfront suites each with deep freestanding tubs and a bunk room ideal for the kids.

The dramatic architecture is softened by a selection of neutral textiles and custom contemporary furnishings and fittings. The outdoor lounge and pool area is positioned for maximum effect with stunning views and uninterrupted solitude.

WHAT WE LIKE

In a dramatic and remote seascape on over 4,000 acres, this award-winning home creates a striking balance within the environment. We love the feeling of absolute seclusion and raw natural beauty.

designed by Andrew Patterson
photos by Annandale

KUCA FOTOGRAFA

Novigrad, Croatia

A Story in Stone

This delightful stone cottage has a great sense of style—and a story to tell. Located in the old town of Novigrad, minutes from the waterfront, it was originally home to wartime photographer Nikica Karavida. When Boris Kajmak, a Croatian interdisciplinary artist and designer, found it, it had been empty for many years. The property is now full of life, with its many original features preserved.

Special attention was given to finding a balance between local architectural traditions (carefully conserved by the local government), local materials and elements of contemporary design.

The house itself is very intimate, and is reached by an internal courtyard that opens up to the neighboring houses, giving it a great sense of community—a bridge between public space and private. We love the exposed beams and stone walls, as well as the wooden floors decorated with splashes of tile, and the upstairs bedroom with freestanding claw-foot tub and wood burning stove.

Guests who are interested in the history of the house will love the photographs on display throughout—all of which were shot in Novigrad by Nikica.

This charming Croatian house is located just a few steps from the waterfront in the old town of Novigrad, Dalmatia and has been carefully restored by a local artist / designer. Once the home of photographer Nikica Karavida, its rustic character and unique story lives on.

designed by Boris Kajmak
photos by Tom de Gay

AAVEGO

Nordjylland, Denmark

AAVEGO

Elemental and Architectural Purity

Designed and built mostly by hand by Danish architect Søren Sarup, this striking compound interacts with the surrounding landscape, integrating the natural and contemporary qualities of simple living. Situated less than a mile from the North Sea around the fjords, lakes and dunes, you can feel a special Nordic bond with nature. The use of light and space both aesthetically and functionally, along with the architectural purity, creates a symbiotic installation that is both dramatic and welcoming.

The warm wood surfaces against the clean white walls and defined edges, combined with a balance of vintage and modern Danish furnishings, creates a calm and relaxed atmosphere on the edge between indoor and outdoor life. The fully equipped kitchen in the main house services both living spaces with interior and exterior dining (depending on weather).

Organized around a large wooden terrace that unites the two structures, the main building and annex can accommodate up to eight guests total. The annex houses four double bedrooms and one bath while the main house features one bedroom and bath and a fireside living area. Each has access to the expansive terrace for places to dine, lounge and enjoy the scenery.

designed by Søren Sarup, puras.dk
photos by Tina Stephansen, Studio55

WHAT WE LIKE

The elemental quality and clean stark architectural lines of these two structures complement the windswept landscape perfectly. Dramatic day or night, the bright interiors and modern silhouettes create a harmonious relationship between environment and great design.

FINIKAS VILLA

Syros, Greece

FINIKAS VILLA

Suspended Above the Sea

On top of a mountain in Kokkina, at the southern tip of the Cycladic island of Syros, this villa is surrounded by olive trees and rugged island terrain, with stunning views over the Aegean Sea and the islands of Naxos, Paros, Serifos and Antiparos. Designed by Athens-based architecture studio, Block 722, the construction blends traditional, natural materials with a zen modernism that recalls the ancient Cycladic forms and style of antiquity. Equipped with state-of-the-art technology, the gated compound still cleverly adheres to an all-natural aesthetic.

A central building houses the living area with stunning views that focus out to sea. The two attached guest houses include two double bedrooms each with private entrances and amazing views and an en-suite master bedroom with an open bathtub and private terrace overlooking the sea. All are serene and private sanctuaries with deluxe baths and easy access to the common areas and pool.

Sheltered by dramatic stone walls, the property features private outdoor dining and lounge areas around the pool that appears suspended over the sea, all aligned with the breathtaking views over Plagia Bay.

This luxury villa in Greece gracefully defines the intersection between modern living and the earthy and timeless characteristics of the islands. With its natural handcrafted materials, serene neutral colors, and simple design concept, the result is a relaxing sense of comfort, style and belonging.

designed by Block 722
photos by Ioanna Roufopoulou

COASTAL BARN

Stokkseyri, Iceland

Along the Volcanic Coast

Along the southern coast of Iceland just 37 mi southeast of Reykjavik, this contemporary home was built as a unique version of a coastal house and gets the tone and style just right.

With views over the rugged lava coastline, the house is ideally situated to explore many of the most amazing landscapes in the south. Clad in weathered timber and created to be eco-friendly, the materials and placement are designed to tread lightly and adapt to the environment with geothermal and hydro-electric power. With a lofty two-story A-frame layout, the interiors are bright and spacious, with the living, dining and kitchen areas sharing the upper floor along with a master bedroom overlooking the coast, and two additional bedrooms on the ground floor. The walls are crafted of branch-less plywood and the floors in rustic planking with a warm, neutral color palette throughout and a spare combination of old world style and modern comforts. With room for up to five guests, the house is ideal for a family or group of friends to share. The surrounding areas feature the best of the raw natural beauty of Iceland with a diverse and peaceful landscape of vast stretches of rugged black sand coast, waterfalls, and glaciers to explore.

WHAT WE LIKE

The outsized proportions and unusual silhouette of this modern barn-style house have a contemporary and rural appeal that suits this landscape perfectly.

designed by Haraldur Björnsson and Rut Káradóttir
photos by Krista Keltanen (p 56) Gunnar Sverrisson (all other)

THE BLACK HOUSE

Borgarnes, Iceland

Icelandic Black and Blues

At the base of mount Hafnarfjall right along the shores of the Snaefellsnes Peninsula, this traditional timber house was built in the authentic 18th – 19th century style of country houses of the region and gets the tone and style just right. Just north of Reykjavik on the western side of the island, you are in a diverse and peaceful landscape of fjords and volcanic peaks along with vast stretches of rugged coast and sea cliffs in a rare and ancient forest from the time of the first settlers. Built entirely of timber, the country cottage is painted in a deep black pitch originally derived from natural tar to withstand the elements. The simple clapboard silhouette is dwarfed by the amazing mountains in the background and matches its environment perfectly.

The interiors are modest in attitude but with a great combination of chic modern personality and old world style designed by Icelandic designer Rut Káradóttir. The lofty open-plan living areas are bright and chic with dark saturated hues that mimic the landscape. With a soaring A-frame layout, the living, dining and kitchen areas share the ground floor with the master bedroom along with a cozy separate loft bedroom at the top overlooking the living room. With room for up to four guests, the house is ideal for a family or group of friends to share.

This is a charming and welcoming house that brings out the best of the raw natural beauty of Iceland.

WHAT WE LIKE

This house perfects its place in the scene with deep, dramatic color within the stark drama of the landscape. Designed after the humble 18th-century coastal houses of the region, this sophisticated update recreates the best of rustic Icelandic culture with a casual mix of 21st-century warmth and refinement.

interior design by Rut Káradóttir
photos by Gunnar Sverrisson

MASSERIA MOROSETA

Ostuni, Italy

Minimalist Masseria

The owner of this property near the Italian town of Ostuni wanted a modern building that wouldn't feel out of place among the ancient olive trees that surround it. To this end, he recruited designer Andrew Trotter to blend the traditional architecture of local masserie with contemporary minimalism. The result is a home that blends old with new—elegant lines with natural elements and rural simplicity. Recycled local sandstone, tufo, has been used throughout, and each room has a vaulted ceiling, with thick, cooling walls.

The structure is built around a central courtyard, and a lovely feature of the property is the high-walled private gardens filled with orange trees (on the left hand side of the house) and private terraces with views of the olive grove. There are many spaces that encourage community, including the living room, veranda, outdoor kitchen and barbecue, spa, gym and large pool. However, if you're looking for solitude, there are plenty of cozy nooks too, both inside and out. The property puts eco-design front and center, with recycled insulation that cuts back on the need for both air-conditioning and heating, windows that allow cross-ventilation, and solar panels that provide enough electricity and heat for the whole building.

The land, and other local growers, provide much of the organic produce that guests are offered for breakfast and at the communal table. There is also a 200-year-old stone oven that's perfect for roasting locally-raised meats and fresh fish.

Travelers looking for a unique destination will love this white stone masseria, perched on a ridge overlooking the sea. It's not only strikingly designed, but it's located in an organic olive grove near the famously picturesque town of Ostuni. It has six generously-sized rooms, and sleeps 14 comfortably.

designed by Andrew Trotter
photos by Salva López

SORRENTO VILLA

Gulf of Naples, Italy

SORRENTO VILLA

Overlooking Capri

Designed by Italian architect Michele Capobianco in 1964, and renovated by Massimo Pica and Ciammara and Alberto Genio, this sea-view villa is not only perfect for lovers of design and architecture , but it is also well located within easy reach of Sorrento, Capri, Pompeii and Napoli.

Perched on a hillside overlooking the sea and the island of Capri, the two-story villa's interiors were designed by Kristine Standnes and feature high ceilings, beautiful tiled floors, with contemporary furnishings and art—from large abstract paintings to imposing sculptures dotted around the property. It's also very spacious, with enough room to sleep up to 10 guests. The first floor has one double bedroom and one twin. Follow the cool spiral staircase, and there's a second floor with a bedroom-studio and a separate guest house has a double family room. Surrounded in parkland, the villa has terraces at ground level and on the rooftop, and a lovely stone-lined pool hangs on the edge of the garden, overlooking the sea. A private stair leads straight down to the beach.

As a location for whiling away the days in the sunshine, reading, swimming and sipping cocktails, this would be very hard to beat.

WHAT WE LIKE

This architectural villa is a showplace of mid-century Italian design with a striking modern art collection and the beauty of the Amalfi coast at your feet. Just a few minutes from the village of Massa Lubrense outside of Sorrento, it's perfectly located to make the most of the region and the stunning views across the Gulf of Naples to Capri.

designed by Italian architect Michele Capobianco in 1964,
and renovated by Massimo Pica and Ciammara and Alberto Genio.
Interior design by Kristin Standnes
photos by Yvonne Wilhelmsen

TORRE PUNTA CAMPANELLA

Gulf of Naples, Italy

TORRE PUNTA CAMPANELLA

Towering Views Above the Sea

Between the Gulf of Naples and the Gulf of Salerno, this villa in Italy overlooks extraordinary views of the island of Capri and the Mediterranean. One of many fortified towers constructed along the promontory, it was placed to communicate directly with the main tower at the point that was the site of the mythical Sirens in Homer's Odyssey. Surrounded by over 500 hectares of National Park land, olive and fruit groves, it's one of several historic buildings on the property that have been transformed into simple and stylish guest accommodations.

Part of a portfolio of properties designed by Naples-based Norwegian architect Kristine Standnes, the home is a successful mix of Italian history, design and culture with a Scandinavian concept and aesthetic. Although the tower's unique configuration poses a challenge in how to interpret the space—with its vertical layout and earthbound materials—the structure comes across as cool, relaxed and unpretentious. Stripped to the bare essentials, the intricate stonework and tile are the ideal backdrop for some cool vintage pieces and decor that neatly coexist.

The ground floor living area comes complete with a fireplace and dining space with a well equipped kitchen and a mezzanine bedroom with towering ceilings and light from the windows above. Up one level is a second living room and bath with the master bedroom above that opens out to the massive platform terrace with panoramic views. The adjacent annex and former olive oil mill is a few minutes walk from the tower with a ground floor kitchen, living room and bath connected by an outside stair to two en-suite double bedrooms with a panoramic terrace. Both homes incorporate several outside dining spaces among the park-like setting.

Throughout the year the owners host an artist-in-residency program focused around the fields of architecture, design, craftsmanship, hospitality and food, designed to inspire intellectual and cultural curiosity and provide a sanctuary where creativity can thrive among nature.

The spectacular Amalfi coast is one of the most iconic stretches of shoreline in Italy and, this 16th-century watchtower commands a magnificent spot above the sea. Standing against the forces of long-ago invaders in the land of Homer's Odyssey, this unique villa in Italy has been restored with a fusion of rustic, southern Italian and Scandinavian inspired design that we love.

designed by Kristine Standnes

photos by Luca Florino (pp 74 & 78 top) & Yvonne Wilhelmsen (all other)

UNPLUGGED IN NATURE

As a child, I loved fairy tales set in farmlands or bucolic villages. For me, there is magic and enchantment in the countryside, where the air is fresher, nature is all around, the old ways still hold, and modernity is on pause.

Living in Hong Kong, one of the mostly densely packed urban capitals in the world, I sometimes find myself overwhelmed, and sometimes exhausted by crowded public places, non-stop electronic communication and socializing. There is a spirit of vibrancy and urgency in cities—so much to see, so much to do, so many ways to spend your money, which though exciting at times, can take its toll, leaving me grouchy and drained.

Whenever I get the chance, I like to escape to the countryside. Pastoral environments seem to lower my stress levels, while increasing my energy, focus and creativity. When I return from a country getaway, my mind is clearer and I am better able to interact with challenging people, find solutions to previously unsolvable problems, and react more calmly to situations like jam-packed subways or long queues at the supermarket.

As a full-time journalist and copywriter, rural destinations help me unplug from work and turn to my own creative projects, like writing short fiction. Being in the country inspires me to look inward and make the space needed for the renewal of body, mind and soul.

Moving at a slower pace, I rediscover the things that make for a good, peaceful and beautiful life—long leisurely walks, landscapes from a Maxfield Parrish painting, dinners that last for more than an hour, the trill of birdsong at dawn, a warm fireplace in the evening, the smell of wildflowers or pine, the taste of freshly baked bread or vegetables from a nearby farm, spotting a hare or a fox in the field, gazing at stars.

I think time in the countryside is particularly important for artists, or anyone who wishes to bring passion into whatever they do. Country living, with its quietude, privacy and wide open green spaces, affords the artist—and shouldn't we all be allowed to be artists?—time to idle and daydream, processes which hectic city life has made almost impossible. This "downtime" I believe, is essential for gaining insight into how to best approach one's work, as it is often during such restful sojourns the muses are awakened.

— Michele Koh Morollo

Michele Koh Morollo is a Singaporean journalist living in Hong Kong. She writes about design and travel for publications like Dwell, Design Anthology and AFAR. She enjoys solo vacations, writing short fiction, yoga, meditation, staying at beautiful properties in peaceful, rural destinations, eating well, and nesting with a pile of good books.

photo by Andrew Morollo

DESERT GOLD

Death Valley, California

Desert Prefab

Located over a hundred miles north of Las Vegas on an 80-acre site in the desert, this home is surrounded by vast expanses of dramatic remote landscape framed by mountains to the north and Death Valley to the west.

Set in splendid isolation, the home was commissioned by the owners and desert aficionados as a unique retreat and was inspired by their first trip to Zabriskie Point. Designed by German architect Peter Strzebniok (nottoscale, San Francisco), the partially prefabricated home is a prototype, constructed in sections and brought to the site to be assembled. Comprised of two complete units, the interlocking sections are slightly raised above the earth, forming a geometric installation of clean lines, and energy efficient wood paneling systems designed with dramatic gold color washes.

Oriented to take advantage of the wind and natural light, the house invites the horizon in, with floor-to-ceiling windows and precise placement. The T-shaped layout is open and bright but compartmentalized with a large living, dining and kitchen area that extends into a spacious deck with a sunken hot tub that can be divided from the rest of the house by the glass doors. The three bedrooms are spacious and bright with alternating views of the landscape and can sleep up to six. Entirely furnished by Mr. Strzebniok down to the tiniest detail, the decor is spare and modern with bright pops of color that reflect the desert palette. Integrating sustainable building practices, the design and materials include alternative renewable energy sources, passive solar design and natural ventilation.

As much of an outward expression as an inspiring and contemplative inward experience, this home transitions and morphs throughout the day, glowing and reflecting the desert light and sky, entirely at home in its place.

WHAT WE LIKE

It takes an adventurous spirit to coexist with the stark extremes of the desert, and this location is as mythical and mind-blowing in its vast, austere beauty as this house is vibrant and lively. We love the dramatic modular silhouette against the landscape and the bright, cheerful interiors that invite the horizon in. Come, and enjoy the middle of nowhere in style.

designed by Peter Strzebniok from Nottoscale
photos by Joe Fletcher Photography

TOPANGA HOUSE

Los Angeles, California

Creative Vintage Beauty

This modern home in the mountains of Topanga Canyon is just minutes away from the beaches of Malibu and Santa Monica and a short drive into greater LA. Surprisingly spacious, the subtle renovation expands on the original footprint of the home creating a bright, open-plan layout with a cozy fireside living room, office and spacious gourmet kitchen along with one large en-suite bedroom and an additional, cozy bedroom nook. The home offers great indoor-outdoor living spaces along with walls of windows, high ceilings, bamboo flooring and striking contemporary and vintage furnishings and decor. Set in a park-like garden with stunning mountain views and salt water pool, there are also two handmade guest cottages that sleep two with separate outdoor kitchenette and dining areas. This is a very chic mountain getaway that embraces style and fun!

WHAT WE LIKE

Chic mid-century design, creative inspiration, and peaceful mountain living come together with great back-to-basics style. Bright, cheerful and eclectic, this home boasts very modern sensibilities with down-to-earth laid-back charm.

designed by Heinz Legler and Veronique Lievre
photos by Laura Austin

TREETOP HOUSE

Malpais, Costa Rica

TREETOP HOUSE

A Lofty Jungle Habitat

Set above the jungle canopy with sweeping 180 degree views of the mountains and the Pacific, this beautiful home is comprised of a trio of "pods" that form a modern and eco-friendly treetop habitat. Designed by Costa Rican architect Benjamin Garcia Saxe, the home has been shortlisted for "House of the Year" by World Architecture News, awarded five Costa Rican Binneal awards and has been featured in Inhabitat, Dezeen, Design Boom, World Architecture News and Su Casa Magazine.

Uniquely designed in three independent sections connected by exterior walkways and bridges, the eco-concious construction was designed for minimal environmental impact utilizing sustainable teak wood, solar power and UV water systems. The large open-plan living room includes a chef's kitchen and dining area and is ideally placed to capture the views with fold away concertina doors that create an indoor-outdoor environment. The wood construction is sleek and modern but warm and inviting with interiors designed by Dante Medri. A lengthy bamboo corridor leads to two upstairs bedrooms with awesome views of the shoreline with a third bedroom downstairs.

The pool is positioned below the house with perfect placement to enjoy the sunsets. Modern and innovative but with an earthy warmth that gently inhabits the jungle environment, this is a luxurious and unique escape.

WHAT WE LIKE

For anyone wishing to try glamping in the treetops of Costa Rica, this house is both chic and eco-friendly and shares its lofty position with the neighboring parrots and monkeys. We love the unique interconnecting pod design, the beautiful teak and bamboo, and the innovative and award-winning architecture that floats above the trees.

designed by Benjamin Garcia Saxe (architect),
Dante Medri (interior designer)
photos by Andres Garcia Lachner

LOS CABOS MODERN

Baja, Mexico

Striking Abstract Minimalism

Perched on a hill above the famous Zippers Beach overlooking the Sea of Cortez, this home in Los Cabos is a one-of-a-kind modern retreat that strips away any artifice, leaving pure structural mastery in its place.

Featured on the cover of Azure Magazine's 10th Annual Houses issue, the home was built in 2014 and is in abstract harmony with the rugged terrain above the town. The property is gated and surrounded by limestone walls and set with a zen space that allows the structure's bold architecture to shine. Comprised of stark whitewashed angles and box forms, the interconnecting interiors are focused around the pool with cool concrete floors and open walls that allow for light and airy open space and seamless indoor/outdoor living. One whole wall is punctuated with colorful tile shared by the living, dining and kitchen area, where you can prepare meals to be enjoyed overlooking the pool. Each of the bedrooms feature separate entrances for privacy and there is a spacious rooftop patio with gorgeous views of the ocean and the sun setting behind the mountains. A perfect place to linger over a glass of wine at the end of the day.

WHAT WE LIKE

Designed with a refreshing minimalism and striking modern style, this Los Cabos home sets an almost dreamlike tone. We love the stark geometric lines that cast shadows throughout the day and the open living areas that flow into one another and interact with the zen garden and pool.

designed by Campos Leckie
photos by Ema Peter

CASA MEZTITLA

Tepoztlan, Mexico

CASA MEZTITLA

El Tepozteco Retreat

Settled at the base of a dramatic outcropping of prehistoric rock formations in an area called Meztitla (which means "place near the moon" in the Nahuatl language), this home lies on the outskirts of Tepoztlán and was created to showcase the extraordinary natural beauty of the site. It was designed by Mexico City-based firm EDAA, who devised an unusual structure that would open out to, as well as blend into, the landscape through an innovative approach to indoor-outdoor boundaries. Constructed of locally sourced lava stone, limestone and concrete, the low-slung profile sits under the jungle canopy with a monolithic box form that juts through the tree tops.

Consisting of four distinct zones, the interiors are composed of a series of interrelated rooms connecting through outdoor areas perpetually open to nature. The L-shaped sunken living room, dining area and kitchen zone feature massive pivoting glass doors that blur the lines even further. The four en-suite bedrooms are located in the center of the house and each have glass walls that immerse you into nature as well as private patios. Upstairs, is an additional studio space with access to the large rooftop terraces. Furnishings and decor are minimalist, with natural fabrics, wood and steel and tropical Mexican furniture such as hammocks.

There is a storm water catchment system devised to provide sustainable year round water for the entire property including the uniquely designed long pool. The property features landscaped terraces constructed over 500 years ago by native Tepoztecos, beneath the craggy El Tepozteco mountains and beautiful native gardens. A stunning accompaniment to the landscape, this house is entirely at one with its surroundings.

WHAT WE LIKE

Designed by Mexico City-based architects EDAA, the expressive modern style and earthy materials of this home create a luxuriously all-natural experience. The massive pivoting glass doors and inter-related spaces form a never-ending relationship with the extraordinary landscape.

designed by EDAA, Luis Arturo Garcia
photos by Yoshihiro Koitani

VERANA

Yelapa, Mexico

Yelapa Bay Views

As you approach Verana from Banderas Bay, you'll first spy the bright orange umbrellas popping out of the jungle. As you get closer, the scene takes shape—a cluster of chic little dwellings with panoramic views of the ocean and the Valle del Sierra Madre Occidental.

Hand-built and carved out of the lush Mexican jungle by Boutique Homes founders Heinz Legler and Veronique Lievre, the hotel is remote and secluded, but still offers all of the comforts for a relaxing and totally unique getaway.

The hotel is accessible only by boat from the mainland, and what it takes to get there (arriving quite stylishly on a mule from the shore!) is nothing compared to what you'll experience when you arrive.

Cited by Vogue as "One of Seven Under-the-Radar Boutique Hotels to Know", the hotel's draw is its unique take on simple luxury among the breathtaking scenery.

Originally intended as a single house, the project grew from the couple's deep appreciation of nature—from images and ideas, and a passion for design and adventure. A wonder of environmental engineering and sheer human grit, the untouched jungle site was carefully shaped and meticulously designed using local materials sourced from the land. It evolved over time into an earthy and stylish compound of nine individual houses, a spa, and a restaurant / bar that serves the freshest of locally sourced ingredients.

Each house was designed with its own character and feel to blend with the environment, and each includes its own private outdoor space.

A special place of spectacular natural beauty, Verana transports you to a private oasis of imagination, artistry and style.

WHAT WE LIKE

It's where the ideas took root and the adventure began... Verana is the place that started it all, and launched what would ultimately become Boutique Homes. Taking you well off the beaten track in a completely immersive experience, it says everything you need to know about our interpretation of modern living and a Chic Nomad's sense of adventure and style.

designed by Heinz Legler and Veronique Lievre
photos by Laura Austin

VILLA YUCATAN

Merida, Mexico

A Dramatic Sense of Space

First place winner of the coveted Cemex Award for both residential and international architectural excellence, this stunning home makes an immediate visual and emotional impact. Designed by Yucatan architect Salvador Reyes Rios, this home uses the latest technologies and techniques to achieve results that are both historically authentic and original in vision.

Located in the small village of Sac Chich in the most historic region of the Yucatan, the home is placed on over two acres of what were once ancient henequen drying fields for industrial production of sisal. Surrounded by the original 10-foot masonry walls of a historic neighboring hacienda that shares the property, the fields are now a massive lawn area lined with royal palms that create a large but very private world all your own.

Constructed using the ancient Mayan technique of chukum, the limestone and plaster are polished to a sleek finish that's elegant and earthy. Entirely open through the middle of the structure, the central living area along with the oversized ceiling and door heights give every room a dramatic sense of space.

With a sunken living room, dining room and fully equipped kitchen, the house is ideal for entertaining and divides the private sleeping spaces to either side. With two bedrooms and two baths it comfortably accommodates up to six. To one side of the house you'll find a patio with a large lily pond and and to the other a beautiful three-sided infinity swimming pool, palapa and patio for dining and lounging.

Designed to highlight the beauty of the Yucatan as well as a unique architectural experience, this is a memorable and luxurious home.

WHAT WE LIKE

The dramatic scale and sublime architectural lines of this award-winning home are in striking contrast to the vast great lawn and jungle that surrounds it. A cool fusion of modern design principles and a faintly Mayan sensibility, we love the inspired creativity and simplicity here.

designed by Salvador Reyes-Rios
photos by Tamara Uribe (p 112) & Pim Schalwijk (all other)

LA GRANGE D'ISIDORE

Brittany, France

A Welder's Barn Reborn

This lovely old barn in the north of France has been given a modern makeover but retains much of its vintage charm.

Part of a complex of holiday cottages, the barn is located in beautiful garden grounds. Its exterior is aged wood with a corrugated iron roof, and this industrial theme continues on the inside. The first floor is an open-plan living area with a beautiful high-gabled ceiling, and sectioned-off master bedroom. An iron staircase and suspended walkway lead to the loft bedroom above. This room is designed for kids, with its three single beds, and whimsical stuffed deer head—but can be used for guests of all ages.

We love the use of natural materials throughout the barn. Exposed or painted stone walls and wooden beams and panelling are mixed with heavy iron railings, and floor-to-ceiling glass. Vintage furnishings and bric-a-brac, splashes of orange and abundant natural light bring the property to life. Large photographs pay tribute to Isidore, the welder whose skills created the ironwork.

The barn is a great location for a romantic country break, but this cottage is tailor-made for a family holiday.

This barn conversion is a striking mix of old and new. A combination of brick, wood, and wrought iron give it a cool industrial feel, but cozy furnishings and vintage pieces create real warmth and character. In addition to looking great, this property is conveniently located for exploring Brittany, and is a great size for a family vacation.

interior design by Liz & Corentin Lamour
photos by Isabelle Le Chanu

MANI TOWER

Peloponnese, Greece

A Peloponnesian Sea Tower

Towards the very south of the Greek Peloponnese is Mani, famed for its old stone towers. If you're craving something different from the Greek islands, and want to stay in an architecturally unique property, it would be hard to find something more interesting than this.

This tower-house, which dates back to the 18th century, is located at Exo Nyfi, an abandoned traditional village, where director John Cassavetes filmed "The Tempest". It looks out over the striking towers of Mani, and is surrounded by olive trees, carob trees and prickly pear cacti.

The tower was recently renovated, keeping the building's traditional style but modernizing interiors with beautiful cave-like lines and minimalist decor. Built into the slope of the hill, the property is divided over three levels, each with access to the garden and yards. The house is made up of two apartments, and both sleep up to four guests.

Rooms are cozy and reach each other by wooden ladders and stone stairways. The house also has an assortment of elegant terraces, offering views of the hillsides rolling down to the sea.

WHAT WE LIKE

Staying in an old Greek tower is appealing enough, but this one has been given a great makeover, turning it into a contemporary cavern.

designed by Elena Zervoudakis, Z-level architecture
photos by Charalabos Louizidis

SIENA LOFT

Tuscany, Italy

SIENA LOFT

A Tuscan Atelier

Just outside of a small village in southern Siena, this former factory has undergone several dramatic changes from its industrial origins. It was discovered by a Belgian couple who fell in love with Tuscany and relocated to create a new hospitality destination.

Built in the late 1960s, it was abandoned until Austrian sculptor and architect Reinhold Traxl created a new living and atelier space, adapting the structure into a box concept. The massive open-plan interiors have been pared down to the original structural metal and wood crossbeams, exposed brick and polished concrete floors with large glass walls that slide away with movable, transparent iron curtains pulling the landscape in. The living area centers around a custom open fireplace designed by Australian artist David McKee creating a dramatic and warm focal point.

Both the kitchen and dining area open into the main room, creating a large unified living space ideal for entertaining. The spaces have been updated with both contemporary and rustic finishes, and a spare collection of colorful and unique vintage and modern furnishings. There are two en-suite bedrooms that can accommodate up to four guests and a shipping container that has been modified to sleep up to two more. Surrounded by nature, the terraces are great for lounging with lovely views of the countryside and the town of Montelifré in the distance. The large lap pool sits among Traxl's stunning garden sculptures and an adjacent old converted electricity tower that now houses a cabana room.

An inspired and chic restoration with an interesting artistic pedigree, this is a unique vacation option in the heart of Tuscany.

Unique in its contrast to the rural beauty of Tuscany, this former factory building has been given vibrant new life and style. Adapted and reimagined over the years by artists, both the lofty interiors and the expansive grounds are modern in tone but with the rustic spirit of Tuscany. We love the massive open-plan living spaces with vintage modern finishes and the monolithic garden sculptures.

designed by Sara Anselmi and Eleonora Crucianelli, margarete.it
interior design by Johny Thielens
photos by Yvan Moreau

SPELLO GARDEN

Umbria, Italy

Village Garden Home

Set within narrow cobbled streets and nestled against the ancient walls of the hill town of Spello, this historic stone villa delivers on charm and style with magnificent west facing views of the Chiona valley and countryside. Centrally located within the town, it's within walking distance of the historic medieval beauty and culture of the village while ensconced within an idyllic and peaceful setting with the heart of rural Umbria at your doorstep.

Restored and redesigned by owner and Spello resident Andrea Falkner, the house is one of three properties she has created as "a home away from home." Built from locally quarried pink-tinted Subasio stone, the ancient arches and stone work provide a palpable sense of history and are paired with fresh contemporary style.

The atmosphere encourages complete relaxation and is decorated with a mix of simple contemporary pieces, antiques and colorful items sourced from Falkner's world travels. The main living area is light and open and laid out to be practical and unfussy with comfortable and cheerful living spaces and chic modern style. The floors are a soft gray resin and the interiors feature bold color blocking and contrasting textures. The kitchen and dining area seats up to eight with a comfy lounge area. Situated on the first floor, the en-suite master bedroom features wonderful garden and countryside views with saturated reds of Morocco while the garden-level blue bedroom is in the spirit of the Aeolian islands with rich textiles, paired with cool white walls, deep blue hues and an old cotto floor. Down the broad stone staircase is the yellow room furnished and decorated with items found in Laos, Cambodia and Burma with private garden access.

The lush and private gardens were designed and planted to allow plenty of space for lounging on comfy day beds piled high with soft pillows or cooling off in the plunge pool with stunning views of the Umbrian hills.

A beautiful garden can complete a home and this historic villa in Spello was designed around the colors, scents and culture of the Umbrian countryside. We love the use of bold colors and natural materials that manage to be contemporary while highlighting the ancient beauty of the Italian landscape. You can almost smell the rosemary, sage, thyme and lavender from here.

designed by Andrea Falkner
photos by Kristian Septimius Krogh

KELLY HOPPEN

FRISIAN FARMHOUSE

Hemelum, Netherlands

Netherlands Meets the Caribbean

The couple who own this home in the Netherlands spent many years living on the Caribbean island of Curaçao, and have brought that relaxed island vibe to this home.

The farmhouse sits on an expanse of farmland in the Dutch province of Friesland, retaining its original character on the outside while its interiors have a cool, modern, bright and airy feel. We love the simple white color palette, and the whimsical, eclectic furnishings—from the free standing wood stove in the living room to the mixed wood and tile kitchen floor, and the church bench that runs alongside the dining table. Other cool features include the elevated tub in the bathroom and the beautiful vaulted ceilings.

With its three bedrooms and two bathrooms, this is an ideal home for a family. The fully-equipped kitchen is perfect for cooking and communal dining, while the large garden has fruit trees and loads of space for children to play. There's also a private terrace, with an outdoor stove, which is perfect for idling away the hours.

This a great location for parties, weddings and other events. For those occasions, the owners open the Sip & Clara pop-up store, which is full of beautiful interior objects and vintage furnishings, inspired by the decor of the farm.

This bright and cheerful former farmhouse in the Netherlands was redesigned and inspired by the breezy vibe of the Caribbean, with striking all-white interiors and sunny, carefree style. A great getaway for a family, there are plenty of spaces for playing and relaxing indoors and out.

designed by Arjan & Rixt Siersma, Claartje Lunter
photos by Hans Mossel

WERELDKAART
JANUS

CASAS CAIADAS

Evora, Portugal

CASAS CAIADAS

Watermills of the Alentejo

Just north of the UNESCO town of Evora in Portugal's rural Alentejo, this cluster of ancient watermills lies in a remote and largely undiscovered region of peaceful countryside.

Named "Most Tasteful Renovation" in Monocle's Travel Top 50 Awards for 2017 and featured in the magazines Wallpaper, Archilovers, Architizer and Archdaily among others, the property was discovered by a Lisbon-based couple and restored in partnership with Portuguese architect Luís Pereira Miguel. An impulsive passion project, the property was designed as an homage to how people once lived and retains all of its original features.

Consisting of three original structures, there is a three-bedroom house with an en-suite master bedroom and two additional bedrooms with a shared bath, and a smaller house that includes one suite. The largest house has a terrace that connects to the swimming pool and offers a large living room and dining area, along with a fully equipped kitchen where breakfast is served daily.

Designed for hosting families, or groups, the property can accommodate up to eight guests and doubles as a hotel in low season. Carefully restoring the ancient structures to retain their authenticity, the ancient stone, timbered ceilings and whitewashed limestone appear much as they were when originally built, with subtle modern updates and amenities. Furnished with traditional handcrafted decor and a minimal aesthetic, the effect is simple, serene and charming.

Surrounded by centennial olive trees, megalithic rock formations and a babbling stream, the property was intentionally kept slightly wild and natural and includes a beach-like swimming pool for cooling off in summer. When night falls, the visibility conditions are like no other place in the south of Europe for star gazing.

These ancient watermills have been rescued from ruin and restored with passion for their cultural significance and simple, rural style. Located in a remote and magical setting, it's as if you've turned back time.

designed by Pereira Miguel Arquitectos
photos by FG+SG architectural photography (p 142 top)
Eugeni Pons Architecture Photography (all others)

COUNTRYSIDE RETREAT

Alentejo, Portugal

Contemporary Alentejo

A family-friendly home designed by the well-known Portugese architect João Favila Menezes, Countryside Retreat has become an important reference point for contemporary architecture in the region, and as such, respects the fundamental principles of traditional Alentejano architecture in its thoughtful construction.

Built on a single floor with windows and patio areas that invite guests to take full advantage of the living space, the house encourages visitors to explore different ways of engaging with the property and the surrounding countryside, but with all of the benefits and comforts of cosmopolitan living. From the rooftop terrace, one can see the historic villa of Monsaraz while taking in the visceral pleasure of living in a world such as this one.

The Countryside Retreat can easily accommodate up to 15 people in four comfortable bedrooms and sleeping areas, and is ideally configured for three couples with up to six children.

The space also includes an indoor dining area, an open-plan living room with fireplace, and a fully equipped kitchen.

The house is surrounded by Mediterranean gardens with three outdoor sitting areas: a cemented patio area near the house with retractable shade-structure ideal for open-air meals, a deck area around the swimming pool next to some of the most beautiful oak trees on the property, and a roof-top terrace perfect for watching the sunset and the stars. Likewise, there are numerous shaded areas under which to rest and take cover from the sun.

WHAT WE LIKE

A striking contrast of bleached exteriors and vibrant colors and decor—we love the simplicity of the architecture and the completely native and wild land that surrounds it.

designed by João Favila Menezes, Atelier Bugio, with gardens by Topiaris Landscape Architecture photos by João Morgado

SIMPLY MODERN BY THE SEA

Comporta, Portugal

SIMPLY MODERN BY THE SEA

Portuguese Seaside

This striking yet simple villa is located near Comporta, Portugal, just minutes from the ocean. Designed by Pedro Ferreira Pinto, it was built in 2010 to blend into the surrounding environment. It features a private terrace with heated pool, pine wood decks, a garden and an interior courtyard.

It may be simple but it lacks nothing in terms of luxuries. Clean lines and large windows afford generous views of the surrounding dune-like fields and native plants.

This spacious (2,850 sq ft) one-story property can easily accommodate six people in one master suite, two double bedrooms and three bathrooms. The living room alone measures 650 sq ft and boasts a suspended fireplace. Its kitchen is fully equipped and built around a central cooking island.

Perhaps the most stunning feature of this property is the rooftop terrace and swimming pool. Measuring 320 sq ft and finished in micro-cement, it is heated year-round, both day and night.

WHAT WE LIKE

This airy and bright villa was designed as the ultimate complement to the the windswept coastal landscape and has plenty to offer—a stunning pool and expansive entertaining decks, and easy access to one of Portugal's best-loved beaches.

designed by Pedro Ferreira Pinto
photos by Andre Antunes

VILLA CP

Girona, Spain

VILLA CP

In the Heart of Catalonia

Set on a hilltop with breathtaking views across the Gavarres mountains and out to the Mediterranean in the distance, this ancient farmhouse was rescued from ruin by Catalan firm Zest Architecture and restored with a vivid and stylish new personality. Surrounded by over 60 acres of private forest and thousands of hectares of protected parkland, it's secluded and very peaceful.

The structure's original rustic appearance was required by Catalan law to be maintained and has been seamlessly restored with its traditional character intact. Set on a slope, the two-story structure's stone façade is punctuated with protruding oversized rusted steelframed windows that capture the incredible views over the landscape that stretches for miles.

The property was designed as a sustainable modern family home, and the architects used Corten steel, wood and hypoallergenic clay instead of plaster as well as cork from the land for insulation, geothermal temperature control and natural water catchment and reed filtration. They significantly enlarged and brightened the interiors, and the upper floor now includes the open-plan gourmet kitchen and dining area with bi-fold doors that open out to the massive upper terrace and gardens and the main living room with a fireplace overlooking the views. Cool and modern, the polished concrete, lofty beamed ceilings, striking steel stairway and minimalist style are paired with vivid textiles and classic mid-century furniture and fixtures that bring it to life.
The four bedrooms are located on the lower level, which is partially sunk into the hill's slope, keeping them cool on hot summer days and sleep up to eight with a separate en-suite annex for two with lovely private views of the forest. All of the bathrooms are fitted with exquisite Bisazza tiles and there's a unique outdoor wet room, lit by punctuated steel doors that open out to the gardens.

The lush grounds are meticulously maintained with native Mediterranean plants and areas for lounging in the hammocks with a shaded alfresco dining and BBQ area next to the pool. Filtered and cleaned by aquatic plants and water lilies, the pool is fed by natural, fresh well water with no chemicals or salt and overlooks the spectacular views. This chic holiday home pairs stylish modern luxury with traditional Catalonian charm in an unforgettable setting.

Striking a lovely balance between old and new, this beautifully crafted former farmhouse has been given a chic modern update that showcases the meticulous craftsmanship and artful use of contrasting materials. We love the simple, understated design that allows the elemental beauty of the house and the knockout views to take center stage.

designed by Co Govers of ZestArchitecture.com
photos by Jesus Granada (p 154) & Jocelyn Mandryk (all other)

LKJ
DUB

&
SCANDINAVIA

SMALL AND BEAUTIFUL

Everyone has their idea of a cabin, some place that's far away and feels a little simpler. It has just the right amount of books, that perfect corner with the view of the woods and the water, that little path you've worn from how many times of coming and going? And that's the thing about cabins that we really love: They're the places we return to. They become our stories, the backdrops to how many summers and how many kids now grown tall? They're possible, attainable dreams that don't cost too much and are usually in some of the most amazing places we can find. Plus, they ask you to slow down, to take a minute and realize that even if you don't have everything figured out, chances are you've got at least the cabin figured out.

Over the years, I've had the chance to see a lot of cabins and to stay in nearly just as many. Seeing that many versions of something so simple is what makes me love the very concept of a cabin even more. They're all so different, absolutely aching for their own twist on what a cabin can be and even should be. They're characters full of inside jokes and winks and they rarely ever take themselves too seriously. They can be stacked log, Japanese timber frame, an exceptionally photogenic A-frame or some wildly experimental design that really couldn't work for anything bigger than a cabin. And that's the fun of it. Cabins can be just about anything. For me, I fell in love with the idea of a cabin before I ever really experienced one. It was the romantic thought of a place far away, probably nestled in the trees, with just enough to get by. A bed, a little stove, a couple knives, a simple pantry—never really anything extra. There's almost always a loft, maybe a table with a couple chairs and a spot to have a fire outside. But then there's my other idea of a cabin that's hyper modern with simple lines and a minimalist mentality.

While I could design a hundred different cabins, they'd all have a common thread of permeability, linked to the nature they're in. I think that's part of the question cabins always answer for me: How can I live just a little better, just a little simpler? More often than not, it's slowing down, and putting ourselves in the way of beauty.

While I don't think I could live in a cabin full time, I do think cabins are the perfect reset button. They're for thinking, getting back in touch with nature, reading, building fires, connecting with people and getting off our screens. It's really no surprise that just about every country has a deeply rooted cabin culture, committed to escapism and connection. Perhaps its our pioneer sensibilities, or maybe it's just because cabins are amazing, but whatever the case, a lot of it really just comes down to having a little place we can call our own.

— Lindsey Bro

Lindsey Bro founded Cabin Love in 2014 and has been a food and travel writer for over a decade. As an expert in content and branding, Lindsey has collaborated with outdoor and lifestyle brands across the industry, sharing the magic and dream of a sustainably adventurous lifestyle. Lindsey has designed and built cabins in both the United States and abroad, focusing on traditional methods with modern style and environmentally conscious practices.

photo by Lindsey Shiflett Smith, Makers Workshop

BASE CAMP

Yosemite, California

Home Base in the Woods

Gently harmonizing with its environment, this back-to-basics cabin provides all of the fundamentals of country living with a touch of contemporary style and modern comforts.

Located above a secluded meadow, the house is very private and surrounded by native forests just minutes away from the south entrance to Yosemite National Park.

The simple clapboard construction and rustic wood interiors are warm and homey while the multiple windows infuse the house with light, framing the wild natural landscape and immersing you into the woods.

The raised platform sleeping nook is surrounded by windows for dreamy nights and the feel of a tree house. With an additional bed, there's room for up to four guests.

The kitchen is fully equipped and you'll have ample space on the large deck with BBQ for alfresco dining and lounging. The fireplace is cozy and warm on chilly nights.

Casual and effortless, this cabin is a great example of relaxing rustic style and easy living.

WHAT WE LIKE

Simplicity, harmony with nature and splendid seclusion make this our go-to cabin in the woods. We love the straightforward rustic/modern profile, warm wood and bright inviting vibe.

designed by Heinz Legler
photos by Laura Austin (pp 161 & 163 top) & Jae Feinberg (all other)

FAR MEADOW

Yosemite, California

FAR MEADOW

The Chic Nomads Yosemite Escape

Far Meadow, as its name suggests, is far off the beaten track—14 miles above Bass Lake in the Sierra National Forest, close to Yosemite National Park.

The beauty of Far Meadow isn't just the 20 acres of private woodland that surround it—it's the fact that it flies in the face of expectations. A collection of three cool cabins, it offers up style more commonly associated with boutique hotels.

Its remote location means that the cabins are inaccessible during the winter, so the two A-frames were prefabricated in the desert then assembled on site. The log cabin, however, is original to the site and just had a facelift.

Individually the cabins sleep between two and four people, but combined they offer accommodation for up to 12. If you need more space still, you can pitch a Teepee Tent for two. And if you think you're really getting away from it all, don't let the surroundings fool you. Far Meadow still offers all the creature comforts you'll ever need, from full kitchens and bathrooms to Wi-Fi.

Far Meadow was brought to life by hoteliers and design connoisseurs Heinz Legler and Veronique Lièvre as "a simple retreat for chic nomads". But it's more than that. It's classic design where you'd least expect it. It's escape without compromise. It's fun with friends. And that includes furry friends too—pets are always welcome.

WHAT WE LIKE

Far Meadow is Yosemite—but without the crowd. Beautiful meadows, wildflowers, amazing sky at night, classic design and creature comforts. Surrounded in acres of private woodland.

designed by Heinz Legler
photos by Jae Feinberg (p 164), Bennet Perez (all other)

CHARLEVOIX CABIN

Québec, Canada

CHARLEVOIX CABIN

Scandinavian Design on Le Massif

Set on a sloped and private wooded site, this cabin in Canada is located in Petite-Rivière-Saint-François, just a few minutes from Le Massif de Charlevoix.

Designed by Quebec City-based Cargo Architecture, the classic A-frame silhouette is undoubtedly modern but was conceived and crafted to complement eastern Quebec's majestic natural beauty. Constructed of pale natural cedar with black metal accents that lend drama and punctuation, the home was developed with the distinctive Scandinavian design principles of clean lines, a pale neutral palette and an economy of gesture.

The soaring gabled roofline lends the interiors a lofty, industrial feel with cool whites, polished concrete floors and bold black-and-white highlights. The layout is spacious and bright with borderless living areas that include a fireside sitting room and a generous dining space adjacent to the sleek, modern kitchen.

Simplicity and functionality were key, with a flow that prompts circulation and carefully positioned windows that frame the landscape from all angles.

Deceptively large, the house can accommodate up to 14 guests with three bedrooms and three baths and a mezzanine area with a private master suite, a child's playroom and additional sleeping areas.

Placed in a forest clearing, the grounds remain all natural where you can enjoy the picturesque views from the sheltered porch swing or from the hot tub après-ski.

WHAT WE LIKE

This modern home in Canada is a visually striking take on the humble mountain cabin. Designed with a stark purity and contrasting natural materials, the Scandinavian-inspired theme is in unique alignment with both nature and contemporary living.

designed by Cargo Architecture
photos by 1Px, Dave Tremblay

LA CASA PEQUENA

Oaxaca, Mexico

LA CASA PEQUENA

At One With Nature

Down a rambling dirt road in what feels like the middle of nowhere, there stands a striking structure that blends a refined modern design aesthetic with a raw, primitive spirit. Just a short distance from the surfing mecca of Puerto Escondido in coastal Oaxaca, the property inhabits a solitary spot in the scrub opening out to a private and wild shoreline all your own. Completed in 2014, the house was inspired by the ethos of Thoreau's Walden Pond and is the brainchild of architect Aranza de Arino and creative director Claudio Sodi.

Constructed entirely of raw concrete with bi-folding wood shutters, the unique residence was designed as a simple modern installation that is as much about design as environment. Towering two stories tall, the house is completely open to the land with the ground floor dedicated to gathering around the huge kitchen table that extends out to the gardens. Upstairs is the ultimate room with a view that sleeps two and downstairs, an open air bath.

Take a refreshing dip in the plunge pool or swing idly in the hammock where you can disconnect and re-charge in a beach house that invites you to escape it all.

WHAT WE LIKE

Raw, unadulterated and entirely at one with nature, we love how two distinct themes can environmentally coexist here. Inspired by Thoreau's call of the wild, this beach house along the Oaxacan coast is a modern homage to simple living that will inspire you to unplug and reconnect with nature.

designed by Aranza de Arino
photos by Camila Cossio

GLASS CABIN

LaConner, Washington

GLASS CABIN

WHAT WE LIKE

Part warm rustic cabin, part modern installation—we love the independent spirit of the design and the rugged location. Life in a transparent home is an amazing and unexpected way to live in the forest by the bay.

Transparent Forest Living

Set on picturesque Fidalgo Island along Reef Point Bay, Glass Cabin is a stunning and imaginative architectural effort. Towering and angular, it nestles into the pines at the water's edge overlooking a breathtaking bay view. This bold transparent structure combines rural warmth and edgy modern style with soaring ceilings and industrial steel beams that frame the interior space while highlighting the dramatic forest setting.

The spacious open-plan living area immediately heightens the senses with walls of glass that slide away allowing nature, light and space to coexist seamlessly. Gleaming pale wood floors and accents offset the geometric angles and contemporary furnishings for a fresh modern interpretation of cabin living.

Anchored with a wood-burning stove and a large family dining area along with the open gourmet kitchen, the living space invites togetherness and intimacy. Tucked away in the eaves upstairs are two simple and comfortable bedrooms as well as a large sleeping loft with geometric skylights and views of nature at treetop level.

The main floor bath is bright and naturally lit with frosted windows that surround you for an au naturel experience. Down the wide outdoor stairs is a stone surfaced patio and dining area with views of Hope Island, Whidbey Island, the Olympic Mountains and beyond. It's the best outdoor space for gathering for BBQs and dining al fresco.

A few steps beyond is your private stair access to the beach.

Glass Cabin is a beautiful forest dwelling that elevates the experience of living in nature and is a graceful and peaceful retreat to the woods.

designed by Zero Plus Architects
photos by Gemma and Andrew Ingalls (p 176) & Thomas M. Barwick (all other)

AUFBERG 1113

Piesendorf, Austria

AUFBERG 1113

Soaring Alpine Views

Although expressly contemporary in design, there's still a nice traditional Alpine vibe here that makes it a rustic wilderness retreat.

Perched high above the valley floor in the pristine High Tauern nature preserve, this home is part of a larger installation designed by Munich-based architect Andreas Meck. Immersed in nature but with warm contemporary style and modern comforts, this home will be your private sky-high nest.

Simple and stylish, the horizontal silhouette and cantilevered design mimics the horizon with walls of south-facing windows to capture the amazing views and the maximum amount of sunlight.

Concrete, pale wood, flagstone floors, and light-filled interiors are stylish but understated for a sense of relaxed living. It's a spacious but intimate two-unit home that can be rented altogether or separately, with ground floor quarters and private bath and an upstairs bedroom with a sliding door that separates it from the main living area. The freestanding tub in the upstairs bedroom affords another great spot to soak in the views, and there's a sauna and spa for warming your bones during the winter. There are two gourmet kitchens at the ready for all your meals.

The free-floating terrace will make you feel the height and affords an unobstructed view all to yourself.

designed by Meck Architekten
photos by Michael Heinrich

WHAT WE LIKE

Clean lines, contrasting textures and raw natural materials have been used to great effect here, creating a modern Alpine getaway. And the view? Breathtaking!

PELLA ROCA
Labastide de Penne, France

Nordic Style in Rural France

On over 20 acres of an 18th-century estate at the gateway to the Quercy Blanc national park, these charming Nordic-inspired cabins are perched within the trees with views over the woods and sprawling countryside. Designed and created as intimate eco-friendly retreats, each of the two cabins are constructed entirely of wood inside and out with clean contemporary lines and rustic charm.

Inside you'll find cool minimalism inspired by Scandinavian design, along with simple rustic modern design that's both chic and homey. Each of the two cabins includes private spas and saunas heated by wood fires and terraces overlooking the countryside and come equipped with a kitchenette and wood burning stove for cozy year round fun.

The grounds include a shared swimming pool, tennis courts a children's playground with trampoline and petanque for true holiday style recreation. Taking an ecological and creative approach to vacation, the owners offer stays designed around culinary and artistic themes with organized truffle hunting, private dinners and guest artists that inspire visitors with presentations of their work.

These cabins in rural France, feature a simple but polished take on glamping and cool Nordic style where you can relax, unplug and enjoy nature among the tree tops.

designed by Camille Arnaud Co design & owners
photos by PELLA ROCA, Cabane & Spa, Gonzalo Botet Photographer

SKYVIEW CABIN

Lettele, Netherlands

SKYVIEW CABIN

Woodland Prefab

Overlooking private forested woodlands and meadows, this modern cabin in the Netherlands is on the edge of what was once a 19th-century hunting domain in the central eastern region of the country.

The first in a series of innovative prefab home concepts, owners and designers Arno Schuurs and Paulien van Noort of the Netherlands-based Qoncepts agency created the cabin as a prototype and show model holiday home. Constructed in two prefabricated sections off site, the parts were transported to and installed on site using an innovative and simple screw foundation technique placing the structure above ground level. Using beautiful, all natural and low maintenance materials including untreated Oregon Pine planks for the façade, oak fishbone flooring, concrete and raw steel, the home is a modern homage to the rustic country cabin.

The smart layout combines a modest footprint that creates the illusion of space, with large windows that blur the boundaries between inside and out and a welcoming sense of warmth and style. The main living area features a sunken lounge space with a fireplace and cleverly integrated built-in custom seating and dining areas along with a fully equipped kitchen. There is one large sleeping area downstairs and a "bird's nest" loft space that can be reached by vertical stairs that is surrounded on three sides by windows and a skylight for star gazing.

Tucked away down a private dirt road in the forest, there are several footpaths on the property that lead to a hammock, a climbing rope, a swing and multiple seating areas for dining alfresco and enjoying nature.

WHAT WE LIKE

This modern cabin in the Netherlands encompasses and incorporates many of our favorite living concepts, with innovative design and construction techniques in harmony with nature, and a stylish and care-free approach to vacation.

designed by Arno Schuurs & Paulien van Noort, Qoncepts
photos by Annelore van Herwijnen

SEA CABINS

Manshausen Island, Norway

Arctic adventure just got a whole lot more modern with these cool cabins in Norway. Conceived and developed by celebrated Arctic explorer and author Børge Ousland, this collection of award-winning sleek and chic waterfront cabins immerses you into the striking beauty of the country through dramatic and innovative design. We love the simplicity, the sense of adventure and the perfect placement.

Artic Archipelago

On the water's edge overlooking the spectacular scenery of the Steigen archipelago, this striking collection of Achitizer award-winning cabins in Norway was commissioned by renowned polar explorer Børge Ousland in partnership with architect Snorre Stinessen.

Inspired to design a unique exploration and adventure resort, Ousland purchased the 55-acre island of Manshausen in 2010, creating a vacation destination and concept that combines the rugged adventure of the Arctic and the striking artistry of modern design. Constructed and assembled on site, the prefabricated structures were designed to limit the impact on the pristine environment and highlight the beauty of the landscape.

Each of the four cabins is placed to maximize the views while providing privacy for the occupants with floor to ceiling walls of glass facing the sea. Three of the four cabins are cantilevered over the stone moorings above the water, while the fourth is set on a rocky ledge at an angle to the coastline. Inside are a double room with main bed ideally positioned to experience the stunning scenery, and a second bedroom which is perfect for kids, or adults.

A restored 18th-century farmhouse was converted into a communal kitchen and dining lounge for guests with an expedition library stocked with books from Borge's personal collection. There are two relaxing hot tubs, a salt water pool and a private beach along with endless wilderness for adventure.

These modern shelters bring out the Arctic explorer and chic nomad in all of us!

designed by Snorre Stinessen
photos by Steve King

TRAVELING WITH FAMILY & FRIENDS

Once a year, I rent a large house in which to spend a long weekend with my friends. It might take a small boat or a train to get there, but we all show up. I like to go to new places with old friends. The plan is to arrive a couple of days early to get the lay of the land and buy local produce. I travel light, bringing only comfortable shoes, a dress I seldom wear and a book I may or may not crack. I buy loads of candles and a bottle of Frangelico or something special to stimulate late night chats, and I make sure there is plenty of firewood, even if it is summertime. Some years there are mountains, some years the ocean and sometimes there are both.

When all the rooms are ready, with crisp beds and fresh flowers, my guests begin to arrive. They come from Long Island and Topanga, Echo Park and San Francisco, Memphis, Tupelo and Scotland. These few days together are for pure joy: talking, eating, drinking, swimming, napping, reading and dancing. Children, teenagers and dogs are always welcome. We will hang out in the kitchen sipping wine and cooking a large pot of chicken and dumplings or seafood pasta, then stay up late telling stories and catching up. Invariably a couple of poems will be read and a few songs sung. I have brought coffee from Memphis and people wander downstairs in the morning at different times when the smell of it brewing fills the house. We snack on fruit and left over baguette from dinner the night before. There are no set plans except to slow down and enjoy.

Even though there is not a birthday to celebrate, I will make a tall chocolate cake that we will end up eating after dinner on the porch and for breakfast on Sunday morning. With a swipe of bittersweet chocolate icing on my fingers and straight to my mouth, I say good-byes, knowing we will meet again next year in another wonderful place we have never been before. I have so often been a guest that I enjoy this opportunity to be the host. As soon as this special annual event is over I immediately begin planning the next trip, searching for the perfect location.

— Terri Phillips

Terri Phillips is an artist and teacher who lives in Memphis, Tennessee, with a passion for road trips, sculpture, her friends and family.

photo by Brian Pera

GEODESIC DOME

Palm Springs, California

Desert Geometry

This thoughtfully restored geodesic dome house sits on a hilltop with mesmerizing desert, mountain, Joshua Tree and Coachella Valley views from virtually every angle, its complete solitude interrupted only by the hypnotic wind turbines that lend an otherworldly beauty to the already dramatic desert landscape. One of three major wind farms in California, the giant sentinel-like windmills stand silently harnessing the power of the wind from the San Gorgonio Pass, rhythmically turning throughout the day and flickering red at night.

Rescued from neglect by LA-based architect Pavlina Williams, this home is a labor of love that has been reimagined from its basic structural roots to a modern showplace with distinctive mid-century styling. The soaring 26-foot ceilings of the dome features a spacious open plan living area with panoramic views from multifaceted windows and the first of three bedrooms in the loft space above. Studded with skylights and the triangular facets of Buckminster Fuller's ingenious geodesic design, the space is a relaxing and dreamy roost.

The ground floor master bedroom has a separate seating area and features amazing views of the Joshua Tree National Park mountains and desert landscape while the third bedroom offers complete privacy with focused views of Mount San Jacinto. There is an office adjacent to the landscaped atrium and a large open kitchen and dining area well equipped for entertaining.

Head out to the covered patio and dining area next to the atrium or sink into the spa and relax under the stars with the city lights of Palm Springs twinkling in the distance.

Escape it all at this fascinating home in Palm Springs. Resurrected from neglect and disrepair by an LA-based architect, this unique compound has been creatively restored with a stylish mid-century inspired aesthetic. We like the fun geometric structural patterns of the dome, the thoughtful attention to detail and the mesmerizing desert views.

designed by Pavlina Williams, AIA
photos by Sam Easterling

FLOATING FARMHOUSE

Catskills Mountains, New York

FLOATING FARMHOUSE

Creekside in the Catskills

Rescued from almost complete ruin, this early 19th-century manor home has undergone a remarkable restoration. (A feature in Dwell Magazine delves into the meticulous mechanics of the restoration and the bio of owner and designer Tom Givone). Taking more than four years of careful work and a complete interior demolition, the period character and bones of the original structure remain intact but with a renewed modern spirit. Set at the edge of a stream with a cascading waterfall, the house is located in one of the loveliest areas of the Catskills surrounded by woods. A study in contrasts, the structure's provincial roots and old world charm are now paired with modern industrial materials and finishes such as steel, glass and concrete. The clapboard exteriors and massive crossbeams were preserved while most of the custom wood work and stone were locally sourced. The large kitchen and dining addition mimics the home's original design, with a wall of skyscraper glass and soaring ceilings. The interiors are minimalist but dramatic in detail with a hand picked collection of vintage and modern industrial furnishings and decor and unique reclaimed items (the 19th-century wood and steel bathtub is a real find!). With five bedrooms and two and a half baths, the house is spacious and can accommodate up to 10 guests with plenty of interior and exterior space for family and friends. Taking full advantage of the beautiful location, the cantilevered porch appears to float on the surface of the water and overlooks all of the high points of the charming country landscape.

This is a home where opposites attract and coexist beautifully.

WHAT WE LIKE

It took an extraordinary amount of imagination, inspiration and artistry to transform this old farmhouse into the polished and modern homestead it is today. We love the contrasts of salvaged and vintage elements paired with modern aesthetics and handcrafted details. It's the perfect synthesis of historic and contemporary design in an idyllic creekside setting.

designed by Tom Givone, givonehome.com
photos by Tommaso Fondi (pp 202 & 205 top),
Marlene Rounds (p 204), & Mark Mahaney, (p 205 bottom)

IL CONVENTO

Corsica, France

Convent Overlooking the Sea

On the northeastern coast of Corsica on the Cap Corse, this former 15th-century Capuchin convent was home to monks before it was acquired in 1796 by a local noble family in whose hands it has remained since. The beauty of the original structure and dedication and passion of the owners to preserve its authentic charm is evident throughout. Classic and traditional, all of the decor, furnishings and original paintings bring back the rich history and timeless appeal. With seven double rooms and three singles, the house sleeps up to 15. Each a timecapsule of history and refinement, some still feature the original layout of the monk's cells. The large country kitchen can serve large groups alfresco and you can have your choice to rent the whole property or come as a B&B guest and enjoy the delicious local cuisine from your hosts. The terraces, solarium and extensive gardens are lush and private and along with the pool offer amazing views of the countryside and out to sea.

We're always discovering something new and amazing in Corsica, and this beautifully restored former convent in the heart of the mountains and the maquis reminds us of why we return every year to our island home.
With beautiful views of the Tyrrhenian Sea, amazingly preserved history and delicious cuisine, we'll be back.

photos by François Cavelier

MAISON DU MAÎTRE & GUEST HOUSE

Quercy Blanc, France

An Expressive Country Estate

On the grounds of a 17th-century estate in the Lot department in Quercy Blanc, this villa is a stylish and sophisticated translation of a historic property. Surrounded by rolling meadows with gorgeous uninterrupted views across the countryside, the main house is one of two private residences available to rent on the 30-acre property, accommodating a total of 14 guests. Featured in Côté Sud and many international design magazines, the property was discovered and restored by an Amsterdam-based interior designer and her partner whose work includes elegant residential projects around the world along with a handcrafted collection of original and innovative furnishings and lighting. Restored with a careful respect for its historic character, the home balances a luxurious sophistication with a casual sense of ease.

The house opens into a double height gallery entry with a spacious open-plan living room adjacent to a dine in chef's kitchen that seats twelve. There's also a separate ground floor lounge and sitting room with doors that open out to the terrace. There are two bedrooms on the ground that can sleep up to four with a shared bath and two additional en suite double bedrooms upstairs. The locally quarried limestone walls, timbered ceilings and rustic aspects of the original house are nicely balanced with designer Kate Hume's eclectic and tasteful decor and finely tuned interiors that bridge the old and new. With dramatic black slate floors and accents, the contrasting colors, texture and striking art pieces are expressive and vibrant.

Outside, the 200-year-old boxwood hedge leads to a private saltwater pool with decks for lounging and grassy lawns that flow into the open meadows surrounding the house.

WHAT WE LIKE

There's something about the striking contrast of dark and light along with the graphic nature of designer Kate Hume's compositions that give this villa in France a tactile sense of texture, mood and modern savvy. It's a seamless adaptation of a historic residence that is equal parts past and present.

designed by Kate Hume & Frans van der Heijden, Amsterdam
photos by Frans van der Heijden

The Meadows Guest House

This guest house is a private companion retreat adjacent to the Maison du Maître. Like the main house, the guest house has been restored with a careful respect for its historic character that balances a luxurious sophistication with a casual sense of ease. Laid out over one floor, the house includes a living room with double height timbered ceilings, a wood burning stove and a large kitchen with an eat in dining area that seats four and a south facing terrace. There are two en suite bedrooms that can sleep up to four with a nice roll top bath in one for soaking. There's also a separate lounge that can double as an extra bedroom.

The main house and guest house together accommodate up to 14 guests.

8 7 6 5

designed by Kate Hume & Frans van der Heijden, Amsterdam
photos by Frans van der Heijden

MAZZINI 31

Umbria, Italy

MAZZINI 31

Umbrian View Palazzo

Just the right amount of luxury and elegance combined with a sometimes edgy injection of contemporary expression and humor make this Baroque style residence a great find.

Faithfully restored from a neglected yet still graceful 17th-century villa, this home's story spans centuries and has now emerged only recently with renewed personality. Hidden beneath the decay was a gem whose transformation retains the best of the original bones and cultural essence.

With a contemporary spirit and a historic heart, you'll find cool vintage items, traditional furnishings and modern pieces interspersed casually throughout for a relaxed unfussy vibe. All of the original frescoes have returned too with the ethereal and mythic imagery reminding you of the home's history.

With three full-sized bedroom suites and four private baths (that remind us of modern versions of ancient Roman baths), there's room for up to eight total, with plenty of privacy and fun individualized design. Expect an understated but no less luxurious version of five-star pampering that includes fully customized meal service from your own Michelin-starred private chefs. The indoor vaulted stone and brick pool room is a great use of, and reminder of, the original house stables that have now become a luxury all season spa, while the terraces are a great spot to dine and soak in the amazing views.

With effortless style and an independent spirit, this home has reinterpreted history.

WHAT WE LIKE

A modern spirit and noble character coexist side by side here, along with breathtaking views of the countryside. Thoughtfully restored, we love that tradition and historic appreciation were as important as personal style. And what style!

designed by Patrizio Fradiani
photos by Bob Coscarelli

PUGLIA MASSERIA

Puglia, Italy

Minimalist Masseria in Puglia

This authentic 16th-century masseria (or farmhouse) in the historically strategic and charmingly traditional location of Puglia, has been painstakingly and beautifully restored by its architect owners. Initially built to resist attacks by invaders, the structure is typical of Puglia, with reinforced stone and brick and authentic historic features. Some original details were lost to time and neglect but have been carefully recreated with accurate authenticity during restoration. Crafted largely of locally quarried tufo, a type of sandstone typical of the area, the vast vaulted stone ceilings cap expansive rooms recreating the historic aspects and detail of the original home. Designed to adapt to the seasons, the thick stone walls and floors keep the interiors cool in summer and warm in winter.

In keeping with the scale of the rooms, the furnishings are minimal and elegant, with both rustic and modern pieces designed to harmonize with the architecture and structure in a smooth balance of old and new. They include handcrafted pottery from the famous ceramics town of Grottaglie nearby.

The main house features a great room with a massive fireplace along with a bright indoor dining area and a modern industrial kitchen perfect for entertaining. Upstairs there are four en-suite bedrooms and a roof terrace with another en suite double downstairs and two additional en suite bedrooms in the adjacent guest quarters. It sleeps 13 guests in total.

Surrounded by organic almond, apricot, pear and fig trees as well as extensive olive groves and vineyards, the property is a vast and productive working farm that is as lovely as it is useful. There is a seasonal vegetable garden that provides the property with goodies for la cucina and two terraces for entertaining and dining al fresco. The pergola covered terrace sits next to the swimming pool and the large sunny courtyard provides additional space with grassy areas and lovely views.

Surrounded by 85 acres of vineyards and orchards, this beautifully restored masseria is a secluded and enchanting retreat. A formerly abandoned ruin, it's now a chic hideaway with an emphasis on culture and nature and an inspiring and serene place of rustic elegance and tradition. We love the vaulted stone work, cool pale palette and simple, luxurious style in and out.

designed by Kristine Standnes
photos by Luca Florino

TORRE DI MORAVOLA

Umbria, Italy

TORRE DI MORAVOLA

Umbrian Tower with Stunning Views

Overlooking magnificent views of the Carpini Valley and the red tiled roofs of Umbrian villages in the distance, this one thousand-year-old watchtower complex is nestled into over six hectares of hillside oak forests, olive groves and orchards with stunning 360-degree views of countryside largely unchanged since medieval times. Originally built to protect the pass through the Carpini Valley and once inhabited by knights, the structures were rescued from ruin by architect Christopher Chong and his designer wife Seonaid Mackenzie. Following years of painstaking restoration, the property was transformed into a unique boutique hotel that reinterprets history for the modern age.

Shoring up the crumbling tower with concrete, steel and stone, the exteriors remain as they have for centuries, while the interiors have undergone an inspired modern renaissance with glass and travertine stone floors, soft neutrals and elegantly conceived additions and materials that mimic the tone and spirit of the ancient structure. The towering silhouette soars to double heights with stairs leading up to communal living spaces and an atrium and includes seven strikingly modern suites arranged around the center. The main suite occupies the top of the tower and features a living area and library on the steel mezzanine and there are two large sitting rooms with majestic ancient fireplaces to cozy up to. The kitchen has been creatively restored and houses the restaurant that serves seasonal and organic locally sourced cuisine following the slow food philosophy. There is an interior fireside dining area but more often than not, you'll want to dine al fresco.

The sprawling gardens are arranged around four terraces with a large formal dining area and a sleek, open viewing pavilion that forms an inner courtyard surrounded by herb gardens. The stone reflecting pool and terrace with sunken seating areas overlooks the olive groves and the large pool boasts spectacular picturesque views of the countryside.

Steeped in history with a vibrant new personality, this extraordinary boutique hotel is a sensory delight where you'll feel completely removed from the modern world. It sleeps up to 18 guests.

WHAT WE LIKE

Meticulously restored and decidedly modern in contrast to its original character, this flawlessly executed recovery of a 10th-century residence seamlessly marries two millennia, delivering stylish modern elegance with a reverence for history and authenticity. Expressive and dramatic, this stunning piece of the past has been brought back to glorious life.

designed by Christopher Chong and Seonaid Mackenzie (MACHNK)
photos by Tribu furniture company (p 230), Pascal Hermans (p 232) & Nicolas Matheus (p 233)

VILLA OLIVI

Marche, Italy

History & Modern Minimalism

A light unadorned approach and simple modern style give this antique home a fresh perspective and renewed personality. Swiss architects Markus Wespi and Jérôme de Meuron have created a stunning contrast of rustic elegance, transforming this traditional country farmhouse with bold contemporary vision and clean straightforward design principles. Spare and chic, the muted earthy tones and sharp white accents have reinvigorated the structural and architectural character uniting history with casual contemporary luxury.

The main house is bright and elegant, with lofty double height ceilings and airy open plan spaces that have expanded and elevated the interiors along with a cozy fireplace. With five en-suite bedrooms between the main house and the guest house, the property sleeps a total of 11 and provides vast indoor and outdoor living spaces.

The sleek state of the art gourmet kitchen can serve up to 12 inside or alfresco on the covered terrace with panoramic views. The outdoor space also includes a kitchen and BBQ for entertaining poolside where you can take in the magnificent landscape.

Refined and elegant, this historic villa will welcome you with simple country living and chic sophisticated style.

WHAT WE LIKE

Fresh, cool and dreamlike, the crisp and modern monochrome palette and earthy rustic structure are a stunning match. Stripped of any artifice, the bare bones minimalist style creates an amazing impact of cool and simple sophistication. And what a view!

designed by Markus Wespi and Jérôme de Meuron
photos by Hannes Henz architecture photographer, Zurich

VILLA EXTRAMUROS

Arraiolos, Portugal

VILLA EXTRAMUROS

Modern Alentejo

Villa Extramuros is a contemporary, five-room property in Arraiolos, a small city in Alentejo, a province famous for its unspoiled natural beauty, long history, and rich gastronomic traditions. Open all year long, the house offers peace and quiet for up to 20 guests in a stunning setting perfectly complemented by clean and modern design.

The villa offers three standard rooms and two superior rooms, all located on the first floor, with panoramic views from their private patios. Standard rooms have separate dressing rooms and bathrooms with showers and natural lighting. Superior rooms offer views of the Arraiolos castle, village and countryside.

Common areas include a living room with fireplace, patio with orange trees, dining room, 50 × 20 ft infinity pool and deck, and two terraces for lounging or dining. The stylish furnishings range from 1950s to the present.

The cuisine is a gourmet mix of Portuguese, Mediterranean, and French specialities, making use of the best of the Alentejo's bounty. Put simply, Villa Extramuros is a chic and elegant property off the beaten track for travelers interested in delving into one of the most beautiful parts of Portugal.

WHAT WE LIKE

An intimate and thoughtfully crafted modern retreat, this off-the-beaten-path boutique home offers just five rooms in a tranquil setting, where contemporary design and simple living coexist beautifully.

designed by Jordi Fornells of Voar Arquitectura, and Rolf Heinemann
photos by Adria Goula & Alex Gempeler

GALICIAN MODERN

Galicia, Spain

Sustainable Coastal Spain

This beautifully crafted award-winning home along the Arousa estuaries in northwestern Spain, has been extensively featured in international design and architectural media and cited as a leader in environmental and energy efficient design. The house was recently awarded the "Most Innovative Contemporary Residential Design" by Build Magazine and "Best Sustainable Architecture" by the Association of Architects of Galicia in 2016. Conceived and designed by Spanish architect Inaki Leite, the home's inspiration was derived from the natural coastal environment and incorporates the beautifully weathered bateas wood from the local mussel fishermen's platforms along with the natural rock faces. The modern, intersecting structural forms have a Scandinavian inspired aesthetic and are clad in the raw, unfinished wood on the exteriors and halved to expose the smooth warm texture on the interiors.

The bright, open spaces are delineated in varying visual relationships and interconnecting living spaces that form striking architectural interaction throughout. The main floor features a large south-facing glass wall with views of the sea and gardens with a fireplace and lounge area and state-of-the-art oak paneled kitchen that serves as the focal point for entertaining and family gatherings. The exposed concrete and folded stainless steel staircase leads to the en-suite master bedroom, with its private rooftop terrace and stunning sea views, as well as an additional terrace bedroom with separate bath. Another stairway leads to the main entrance and two ground floor bedrooms. It sleeps eight guests.

Along with the locally sourced materials, every element in the home was handmade by local craftsmen including the gorgeous bespoke furnishings and finishes. Carefully designed with respect for nature and environmental impact, the home received the highest energy efficient rating through a series of complex solar, insulation and ventilation systems and a purifying vertical moss garden installed with the help of a renowned Spanish botanical biologist. Just steps from the shore, this modern beach house is an inspired work of art.

WHAT WE LIKE

The remarkable composition and creativity of this award-winning coastal house is an inspired modern tribute to northern Spain's natural beauty. Incorporating authentic Galician character, and thoughtfully crafted with respect for the environment, the striking architectural geometry, raw materials and bespoke interiors are masterfully designed.

designed by Iñaki Leite
photos by Adrián Vázquez

MALLORCA VILLA

Mallorca, Spain

Mallorcan Minimalism

Set in an almond grove on the southern part of the island, Mallorca Villa was designed by John Pawson and Claudio Silvestrin, the duo responsible for designing leading retail locations for Calvin Klein and Giorgio Armani. With stunning views of the sea and the mountains, it is a highly expressive and unusual structure, and a daring leap into what a residential space can mean.

Grand in scale and humble in tone, the house is reminiscent of an art installation, and its clean sharp delineated lines of vertical and geometric shapes evoke a modern take on antiquity. Equal parts mid-century modern and ancient adobe castle, the striking minimalist emphasis in and out and use of raw, natural materials create a harmonious palette with the landscape.

With over 6,000 square feet, this spacious home features five bedrooms with one master, that sleep a total of 11. Each is completely unadorned and refreshing in its simplicity while still remaining luxurious. The fully equipped kitchen and adjoining dining area are large enough to serve up to 10 and are adjacent to the expansive pool terrace and indoor courtyard for great open air living. There is a rooftop terrace and two additional wrap-around terraces for lounging. Along with the 100-foot infinity pool there is an additional pool underneath with a waterfall that has a walled area for children and a sunken tennis court. With over 30 acres of expansive gardens, the property is in complete, secluded privacy.

With an unusual economy of design, this villa is nevertheless a vivid and stylish statement.

WHAT WE LIKE

Zen and dreamlike, this is a daring example of less is more. We loved the dramatic geometric lines and complete lack of ornamentation which let the architecture and the landscape shine.

designed by John Pawson and Claudio Silvestrin
photos by Albert Neuendorf (p 252 top) & Michael Pentzien (all other)

David Hockney

ON THE PULSE OF CULTURE

Quiet is for the unconscious hours, when one is asleep or under general anesthesia. Isn't it possible that serenity is a euphemism for boredom or stagnation? That it's much more exciting, maybe even useful, to be awake, alert and hammered by the senses?

Nature has the reputation of recharging the spirit, but really, a city can offer much more energy to feed from. Nature is salad. A city is carbs and sugar and protein. It's satisfying, varied, maybe it leads to some discomfort, but it's worth it. Take an antacid. Get on with it.

Visiting a new city, particularly one with a healthy (or charmingly unhealthy) social and cultural life, can remind you how much you don't know, how much you will never know, how big and impressive the world is beyond your subjective experience in it. Even without the use of a guide or tour, simply existing elsewhere, for however long your schedule permits, saturates the soul with architecture, art, history, different languages, different rituals and movements, gesticulations, politics and dramas. Much better to get lost in an unfamiliar neighborhood than in one's own thoughts ... we spend enough time with those anyway.

We tend to venerate the relationships we build across the world when we travel, but the occasional antisocial moment in an extroverted city is just as valuable. How cinematic to stand on a third-story balcony and allow your eyes to follow the traffic moving past living room windows; to sit alone at a café and pretend to read a book while eavesdropping on a conversation you barely understand; to wake to the sound of a neighbor coughing over a morning cigarette rather than a rooster crowing.

For those who wish to get outside themselves, the city offers distraction and the engrossing adrenaline of novelty and change. For those who wish to find themselves, nothing brings one's awareness inward more than having to navigate an unfamiliar public transportation system or social situation, or having to avoid an allergen on a menu in an unknown language. Looking up to see the stars at night is certainly breathtaking. So, too, is drowning in the light pollution of a city in which thousands, even millions of different lives exist alongside your own.

— Katya Tylevich

Katya Tylevich is co-author of the book "My Life as a Work of Art" (Laurence King, 2016) with Ben Eastham, Editor-at-Large for arts journal Elephant, Contributing Editor for Mark, and a contributor to Domus, Pin-Up and Frame, among other journals. She has written for the books and exhibitions of many artists, including Todd Hido, Michaël Borremans, Espen Dietrichson and Doug Aitken. With her brother Alexei, she is co-founder of Friend & Colleague, a platform for fiction and special projects.

photo by Alexei Tylevich

LA FUENTE APARTMENT

Mexico City, Mexico

Inside Roma Norte

In a contemporary building on a quiet street in Roma Norte, this stylish home in Mexico City is immersed within a lively and artistic neighborhood just west of the city center.

Designed in cool urban style, the interiors are a neutral gray with contrasting design details and decor that add color and contemporary glamour.

The sitting room overlooks the streets below with floor-to-ceiling windows and a small terrace that allow in natural light without sacrificing privacy. The fully equipped modern kitchen includes a dining area for four and a central hall of glass divides the space from the two double bedrooms located at the back of the apartment.

Tastefully decorated with contemporary furnishings and decor, this urban retreat is equipped with both style and comfort.

This stylish home in Mexico City is a modern urban retreat in a neighborhood alive with artistic energy. We like the calm, neutral interiors, abundant light and eclectic design details.

designed by Christian Sarubi
photos by José Margalef

MESON SAN SEBASTIAN

Merida, Mexico

MESON SAN SEBASTIAN

Colonial Merida

This home in one the oldest barrios of Merida's historic colonial center is the brainchild of a pair of expats who discovered the city in the early 2000s and have since renovated over a dozen properties throughout the area. The duo's past in the world of fashion, interior design and fine arts is evident in the restoration as well as the tasteful and simple luxuries of each of their homes.

Infusing the ancient structure with a modern and laid-back vibe, the soaring interiors feature burnished plaster walls and polished concrete floors and are awash in natural light from multiple skylights. The open and airy floor plan includes a large living room at the front of the house with another sitting room that opens onto an amazing garden and pool terrace—unusual for a townhouse in these parts. There is a formal dining room as well as an informal dining area adjacent to the fully equipped kitchen with plenty of room for entertaining. The three double bedrooms are at the back of the house which include two guest rooms and the master suite that can accommodate a total of six guests.

As avid collectors of crafts and antiques, the owners have filled the house with an eclectic mix of modern and vintage furnishings, with both rustic local pieces and a few Baroque touches thrown in.

One of several homes restored and redesigned by a pair of American expats, this property in Merida is a uniquely fashionable and respectful recreation of one of the city's original colonial gems. We like the interesting mix of furnishings and decor against the backdrop of limestone and concrete. The oasis-like pool and gardens are a special treat for city dwellers.

designed by John Prentice Powell
photos by Neil Youngson

CITY PENTHOUSE

Tasmania, Australia

CITY PENTHOUSE

Hobart Sky Views

"This City Penthouse will be a striking new addition to the city" (Gourmet Traveller Magazine). And indeed, this modern and welcoming retreat is an oasis of surprise and inspiration. Sitting atop a nine story office tower, the penthouse enjoys grandstand views of the city, the park, Salamanca River and the distant horizon beyond.

The location combines easy access to the waterfront so you can catch the ferry to MONA or enjoy the Salamanca Restaurants. This exciting cantilevered modular designed penthouse with all the beautiful details has a very personal sensibility.

The City Penthouse has two bedrooms and two en-suite bathrooms and sleeps four people. There is a fully stocked gourmet kitchen with Scholtes appliances.

An artisan Huon pine table has enough room for up to 10 people and makes the perfect location for a memorable meal overlooking spectacular city views.

designed by Peter Willmott
photos by Jonathan Wherrett

WHAT WE LIKE

With decks on both sides, it's hard to beat the views. Take in the sunrise on one side and the sunset on the other. Lifted and suspended atop an office building, this prefab omnipod feels like it's floating above the city or a cruise ship in the sky. Super cool.

ATELIER APARTMENT

Vienna, Austria

ATELIER APARTMENT

Vienna Artist's Atelier

In a beautiful historic building in Vienna's elegant and vibrant 18th district, this apartment once served as both a crafts shop and artist atelier. Discovered and redesigned by the founder of design firm VIVIDGREY, the apartment features a generous open floor plan and a range of exquisite handmade textiles, locally handcrafted furniture and original artwork.

Accessed via a communal front garden and private entrance—a rarity in Vienna— the steps lead down into a bright open space with vaulted ceilings and a drawing room with a day bed and sofa lounge area. At the rear end of the space, a large double bed is screened off by a low level wall with an integrated dressing area. A separate bedroom facing the quiet back garden of the building has two standard single beds and can either be arranged as a children's room or as another double bedroom.

Leading off the main room, the spacious kitchen features a large dining table with seating for four.

WHAT WE LIKE

Atmospheric and sophisticated, but with a family-friendly informality, this apartment features the expressive, handcrafted work and unique style of the owner's exclusive home furnishings and interior design line. We love the soothing monochromatic palette, punctuated with texture and the chic and unusual design accents.

designed by Sabine Fajana / VIVIDGREY
photos by Sabine Fajana / VIVIDGREY

ANTWERP DESIGN APARTMENT

Antwerp, Belgium

Life & Culture in Antwerp

This hybrid concept in the vibrant center of Antwerp encompasses the arts of design, fashion, culture and gastronomy under one roof.

Conceived and designed by a Belgian couple who initially called the space home, this townhouse has been transformed into a specialty destination that includes a restaurant, a design shop, an art gallery and a chic upper apartment.

The building's traditional neoclassical features and historic facade remain while the interiors were completely redesigned by Vincent Van Duysen, one of Belgian's most renown architects. Chic and atmospheric, the spaces are modern but welcoming and softened by natural materials. The soothing monochromatic and elemental design still manages to pique your senses but with a feeling of ease and harmony.

Divided over two floors, the apartment includes a large fireside living space and dining room, a fully equipped kitchen and a large terrace overlooking the historic city center. Each floor is flooded with natural light and looks out onto a picturesque square where the trees reveal the passing of the seasons.

With four bedrooms, and two baths, the apartment can accommodate up to six guests.

The award-winning restaurant serves only the best of what's local and fresh, with ingredients harvested daily and seasonally into light and healthy taste sensations.

The first floor exhibition space is an inspiring and multipurpose location that also functions as a platform for supporting up-and-coming art and fashion talent, while the in house boutique features a rotating collection of stylish high-end fashion, curious design objects and collectibles sourced from around the world. All of the items are carefully curated and selected by the owners along with art director Bob Verhelst. Described as "their best kept secret," this remarkable concept allows you to live in and enjoy the striking design, the delicious cuisine and the creative wonder of this ongoing project.

There's something both comforting and bold about the pared down absence of things, the purity of space and design and the concept of less is more that makes a lasting impression. This is where fashion, art, gastronomy and cultural expression come to life in Belgium's cool second city.

designed by Vincent van Duysen, graanmarkt13.com
photos by Frederik Vercruysse

PARISIAN LOFT

Paris, France

The Railway Loft

This spacious apartment is in central Paris, adjacent to the Gare de l'Est. The building it occupies is a former warehouse dating back to 1850, which sheltered the archives of the SNCF (French National Railway Company).

Today it has been refurbished and converted into apartments. This loft is located on the upper floors and retains much of its original charm, with features like the staircase and the bookcase preserved.

The property is accessed by a private glass elevator which soars alongside one of the biggest vertical gardens in the world. In spite of its central location, the apartment is peaceful in the daytime and at night.

An immense teak footbridge, shared by the lofts, serves as a terrace, and is furnished with armchairs, chairs and tables.

The loft is 23-feet high and split into two levels: second floor and mezzanine. The lower level holds a lounge, open kitchen, bathroom (under the staircase) and toilets. The mezzanine has a bedroom, office and two dressing rooms. The latter faces the plant wall, which guests can watch from the bathtub.

WHAT WE LIKE

This city-center loft is located in a fantastic converted 19th-century railway warehouse that blends traditional and modern aesthetics with flair. We love the striking vertical garden that adorns its walls.

designed by Paul-Adrien Gouny & Bernard Crouzet
photos by Martin Nicholas Kunz

BRUNO TAUT HOUSE

Berlin, Germany

Pioneering Modernism in Berlin

This home in the southern Britz district of Berlin is part of one of the world's most influential residential developments, conceived and designed by architect Bruno Taut. Winner of the European Union Prize for Cultural Heritage and a designated UNESCO World Heritage site, the development was completed by Taut and urban planner Martin Wagner in 1924. Designed in a dramatic horseshoe shape and surrounded by symmetrical rows of townhouses, the installation was created as an idyllic answer to the more oppressive prewar style with extensive garden spaces and an entirely new approach to traditional residential design.

The owners of the house—a specialist in cultural and contemporary history, and a garden and landscape architect specializing in monument sites—are the ideal stewards of the property and have lived at the site for almost two decades. Passionately committed heritage conservationists, the couple have completely and carefully restored the house with authentic 1920s style and historically accurate design detail.

Recalling both the Bauhaus and International themes, the house features clean, angular lines with an emphasis on light and air and is embedded within a charming urban garden.

The clever layout manages to fit a lot of style and livability into a compact space. The main living room with its mint green walls and matching enamel fireplace is intimate and simple with a dining area that sits off of the kitchen—a well equipped replica from another Taut house nearby, with original fittings and views of the gardens. The two double bedrooms upstairs are bright and almost zen like in their simplicity with lively blue and yellow color washing, classic vintage style and treetop garden views.

All furnishings, fixtures and decor are restored originals or made to measure from vintage 1920s models adding to the charm, authenticity and nostalgia. The large yard and gardens have also been restored according to the original blueprint with a small terrace surrounded by fruit trees, lilac bushes and wild roses.

WHAT WE LIKE

This award-winning and carefully preserved home is a time capsule of style that captures an important architectural movement and its ideals with simple, but striking design. It appears untouched by time, and is a unique opportunity for design enthusiasts to experience a vintage modern home as it was originally intended. This is a museum meant to be live in.

designed by Bruno Taut
photos by Martin Nicholas Kunz (p 285) & tautshome.com (all other)

Zuck
Kaff
Tee

Topflappen

RIVERVIEW SUITE

Verona, Italy

RIVERVIEW SUITE

Vintage Verona

Set directly along the Adige River in the heart of Verona, this 17th-century former palace houses a uniquely restored apartment suite ideal for two. Developed in collaboration with Milan-based architect Stefania Beltrame, the owners were inspired by their experiences traveling the world exploring some of the most curious and stylish places to stay and wanted to create a unique modern hideaway with vintage appeal. Working with some of the best local craftsmen, they conceived contemporary custom furnishings to accompany original vintage furnishings by Osvaldo Borsani, Silvio Cavatorta, Vittorio Nicolis and Marco Zanuso with luxurious Italian marble, brass and boiserie finishes and gorgeous custom wallpapers by Fornasetti, Cole & Son and Elitis-Soie.

Compact but spaciously laid out, the interiors are divided by glass, curtains and mirrors instead of fixed walls, creating an active space that can be adjusted according to your mood and needs.

The double "bedroom" faces the unique glass bath and shares the open plan space with a small well appointed kitchen with dining for two. The state of the art technology is cleverly integrated with the chic design, striking a harmonious balance between style and comfort.

designed by Stefania Beltrame, Beltrame-Gelmetti Studio, Milan
photos by Filippo Turco

WHAT WE LIKE

This is a richly detailed and beautifully designed river front home in the heart of Verona with an intricately balanced sense of modern comfort and vintage style. We love the authentic mid-century Italian pieces, the colorful custom furnishings and wallpapers and luxurious materials.

TORINO PENTHOUSE

Torino, Italy

TORINO PENTHOUSE

Turin Factory Conversion

Walls of windows and blasted brick, polished concrete floors and soaring ceilings, instantly remind you that this was once a working factory. A cool and exhilarating renovation has stripped the raw space and light down to their most elemental, while incorporating a new geometric aesthetic, creating a very modern and elegant residence. Minimal in tone and style, the simple color palette is repeated throughout the home with occasional bursts of primary colors that accent the muted design.

Designed and completed by the prestigious UdA, this was a complete interior and landscape update. Bright and serene, the main floor is light filled and open to the spare, fully equipped kitchen and dining area that serves eight. Black lacquered accent walls create a dramatic architectural statement and focal point that leads to the upper floors.

The double height master bedroom is a private retreat set high atop the building with private en suite bath, independent from the additional studio bedroom by separate stairways. Each has two full baths and shower rooms, that are sleek and modern. Beautiful, specially selected vintage and contemporary furnishings and art complete and complement the creative vision of the architectural restoration and design.

And finally, the rooftop terrace affords unobstructed panoramic views of the city and is a secluded oasis to sunbathe (with an out-door shower).

A perfect hideaway and base for a great experience in one of the most beautiful and avant-garde towns in Italy, Torino Penthouse is a ideal destination to enjoy this fascinating city.

Torino Penthouse is a stunning example of great vintage renovation and use of space. All light, height and neutral colors, the overall effect is an elegant, utilitarian and design centric renewal.

design by Max Camoletto & Susanna Cucco
photos by Max Zambelli

APARTMENTS ON THE DOURO

Porto, Portugal

WHAT WE LIKE

The beautiful city of Porto in northern Portugal is often referred to as Cidade das Pontes —or the City of the Bridges. And this property pays homage to this nickname. It's a collection of six minimalist contemporary apartments named after the city's six famous bridges and features stunning views over the rooftops, the river and the bridges.

designed by Hugo Ferreira & Nuno Sousa
photos by João Cruz, WOW Brand Energisers (p 299 top) & José Campos (all other)

Cidade Las Pontes

These six apartments are on the banks of the River Douro near the Dom Luís Bridge. A double-decked metal arch designed by Teophile Seyrig, a student of Gustave Eiffel, the bridge opened in 1886 and spans the river between Porto and Vila Nova de Gaia, and is now a UNESCO World Heritage Site.

This setting inspired the names of these six minimalist, modern apartments. The largest is D. Luís itself, which is ideal for families, two couples or a group of friends. The bridge has two decks, and this apartment has two bedrooms with room for six guests, as well as a deck with a stunning view of Porto.

Da Maria is the smallest of the apartments, with one bedroom that sleeps two guests. S. João, Freixo Arrábida, and Infante all have one bedroom with enough space for four guests, and each apartment has a bathroom and a kitchenette. Design-wise, the apartments couldn't be simpler. Bare wood, concrete, utilitarian furniture, no clutter, no frills, with breathtaking views and an unbeatable location.

EL RASTRO

Madrid, Spain

Madrid Market Apartment

This newly restored 18th-century apartment in the bustling El Rastro district of central Madrid has been modified and updated with an invigorating contemporary energy and chic Bohemian style. Known as "corrala madrilen", the building is one of many traditional townhouses in the area that feature charming historic apartments with balconies positioned around a central courtyard. Next to La Latina, Plaza de Cascorro and the famous calle Ribera de Curtidores, the area is also home to Madrid's most famous and symbolic outdoor market, el Rastro.

The bright open plan interiors have been pared down to the original structural spaces with exposed wood crossbeams, high ceilings and bright airy interiors. Updated with both contemporary and rustic finishes, the apartment is warm and welcoming with a chic and understated collection of unique and colorful vintage modern furnishings. The main living area overlooks the courtyard and flows into the fully equipped eat-in kitchen.

A glimpse into modern Madrid, this apartment also has an inspired bohemian spirit that allows travelers to enjoy the energy and culture of the city.

WHAT WE LIKE

There's a rustic warmth and authenticity to this urban apartment that we love. Restored to salvage the original character and charm of early 18th-century Madrid, the weathered patinas and cool vintage style are creatively paired with a fresh, modern update.

designed/renovated by Paco Ruiz-Nicoli
photos by Pedro de Agustín

Produced by COOL CITIES MEDIA GMBH, BERLIN 2018
Curated by Heinz Legler, Veronique Lievre, Martin Nicholas Kunz

Copyrights for texts and photos see credits
Texts: Nancy Bachman, Lindsey Bro, Mary Douris, Heinz Legler, Léonard Lièvre, Michele Koh Morollo, Roshan McArthur, Terri Phillips, Katya Tylevich
Copy Editing: Mary Douris, Roshan McArthur, Nicholas Thompson
Editorial Management: Mariana Campbell, Paulina Cervantes, Betti Fiegle
Art Direction and Layout: Mareike Walter
Layout Assistance: Betti Fiegle
Photo Editing: Betti Fiegle
Imaging: Heiko Pense

1461 Brookings Trail, Topanga, California, 90290
e-mail: hello@boutique-homes.com
www.boutique-homes.com

Kohlfurter Straße 41–43, 10999 Berlin, Germany
Phone: +49 (0)30 / 89 40 56 77
e-mail: info@cool-cities.com
www.cool-cities.com

International Distribution:
avediton GmbH
Publishers for Architecture and Design
Senefelderstraße 109, 70176 Stuttgart, Germany
Phone: +49 (0)711 / 2 20 22 79-0
e-mail: contact@avedition.de
www.avedition.com

ISBN: 978-3-89986-274-4

Printed by Liberduplex, Barcelona

Photocredits:
p 05 Laura Austin, lauraaustinphoto.com; p 06 Eva Napp, evanapp.com; p 09 Antoine Lièvre; pp 10–13 (Schoolhouse) William Green, williamgreen-photography.com; pp 14–17 (Holbox Island Bungalow) Marco Badalian, kuaphotography.com; pp 18–21 (Palapa Beach House) Brian Hodges, brianhodgesphoto.com; pp 22–25 (Neskowin Beach House) ingallsphoto.com; pp 26–29 (Coastal Glass House) Jonathan Wherrett, jonathanwherrett.com; pp 30–35 (Pigeon Bay) Simon Devitt, simondevitt.com; pp 36–39 (Scrubby Bay) Annandale; pp 40–45 (Kuca Fotografa) Tom de Gay, tomdegay.com; pp 46–49 (Aavego) Tina Stephansen, studio55.dk; pp 50–55 (Finikas Villa) Ioanna Roufopoulou, ioannaroufopoulou.gr; pp 56–59 (Coastal Barn) Krista Keltanen, kristakeltanen.com & Gunnar Sverrisson, gunnarimage.com; pp 60–63 (The Black House) Gunnar Sverrisson, gunnarimage.com; pp 64–67 (Masseria Moroseta) Salva López, salvalopez.com; pp 68–73 (Sorrento Villa) Yvonne Wilhelmsen, yvonnewilhelmsen.no; pp 74–79 (Torre Punta Campanela) Luca Florino, lucaflorino.com & Yvonne Wilhelmsen, yvonnewilhelmsen.no; p 81 Andrew Morollo; pp 82–85 (Desert Gold) Joe Fletcher, joefletcherphoto.com; pp 86–91 (Topanga House) Laura Austin, lauraaustinphoto.com; pp 92–95 (Treetop House) Andres Garcia Lachner, garcialachner.com; pp 96–99 Ema Peter, emapeter.com; pp 100–103 (Casa Meztitla) Yoshihiro Koitani, kuu.vision; pp 104–109 (Verana) Laura Austin lauraaustinphoto.com; pp 110–113 (Villa Yucatan) Pim Schalwijk, aventuramexico.com.mx & Tamara Uribe, tamarauribe.com; pp 114–117 (La Grange D'Isidore) Isabelle Le Chanu, imagezvous.com; pp 118–123 (Mani Tower) Charalabos Louizidis; pp 124–129 (Siena Loft) Yvan Moreau, yvanmoreau.com; pp 130–133 (Spello Garden) Kristian Septimius Krogh, septimiuskrogh.dk; pp 134–137 (Frisian Farmhouse) Hans Mossel, hansmossel.nl; pp 138–143 (Casas Caiadas) Eugeni Pons, eugeni-pons.com & FG+SG architectural photography, ultimasreportagens.com; pp 144–147 (Coutryside Retreat) João Morgado, joaomorgado.com; pp 148–151 (Simply Modern by the Sea) Andre Antunes; pp 152–157 (Villa CP) Jesus Granada, jesusgranada.com & Jocelyn Mandryk, jocelynmandrykphoto.com; p 159 Lindsey Shiflett Smith, Makers Workshop; pp 160–163 (Base Camp) Jae Feinberg, jaefeinberg.com & Laura Austin, lauraaustinphoto.com; pp164–167 (Far Meadow) Jae Feinberg, jaefeinberg.com & Bennet Perez, bennetperez.com; pp 168–171 (Charlevoix Cabin) Dave Tremblay, onepx.ca; pp 172–175 (Casa Pequena) Camila Cossio, camilacossio.com; pp 176–179 (Glass Cabin) Gemma and Andrew Ingalls, ingallsphoto.com & Thomas M. Barwick, barwickphoto.com; pp 180–183 (Aufberg 1113) Michael Heinrich, mhfa.de; pp 184–187 (Pella Roca) PELLA ROCA, Cabane & Spa – Gonzalo Botet, gonzalobotet.com; pp 188–191 (Skyview Cabin) Annelore van Herwijnen, annelore.nl; pp 192–195 (Sea Cabins) Steve King, stevekingphoto.com; p 197 Brian Pera; pp 198–201 (Geodesic Dome) Sam Easterling, thewildeast.co; pp 202–205 (Floating Farmhouse) Mark Mahaney, markmahaney.com & Marlene Rounds, marlenerounds.com & Tommaso Fondi; pp 206–211 (Il Convento) François Cavelier, francoiscavelier.com; pp 212–219 (Maison Du Maitre & The Meadows House) Frans van der Hejden, heijdenhume.com; pp 220–223 (Mazzini 31) Bob Coscarelli, coscarelli.com; pp 224–229 (Puglia Masseria) Luca Florino, lucaflorino.com; pp 230–233 (Torre di Moravola) Nicolas Matheus, matheusphoto.com & Pascal Hermans, pascalhermans.nl; pp 234–239 (Villa Olivi) Hannes Henz, hanneshenz.ch; pp 240–243 (Villa Extramuros) Adria Goula, adriagoula.com & Alex Gempeler, architekturfotografie.ch; pp 244–247 (Galician Modern) Adrián Vázquez, adrianvazquez.carbonmade.com; pp 248–253 (Mallorca Villa) Albert Neuendorf, albertndf.tumblr.com & Michael Pentzien, ahoygallery.com; p 255 Alexei Tylevich; pp 256–259 (La Fuente Apartment) José Margalef, josemargaleff.com; pp 260–265 (Meson San Sebastian) Neil Youngson, yucatanlight.com; pp 266–269 (City Penthouse) Jonathan Wherrett, jonathanwherrett.com; pp 270–273 (Atelier Apartment) Sabine Fajana, sabinefajana.com; pp 274–277 (Antwerp Design Apartment) Frederik Vercruysse, frederikvercruysse.com; pp 278–281 (Parisian Loft) Martin Nicholas Kunz, martinnicholaskunz.com; pp 282–285 (Bruno Taut House) Martin Nicholas Kunz, martinnicholaskunz.com & tautshome.com; pp 286–289 (Riverview Suite) Filippo Turco; pp 290–295 (Torino Penthouse) Max Zambelli, maxzambelli.com; pp 296–299 (Apartments on the Douro) João Cruz, wowagency.pt & José Campos, josecamposphotography.com; pp 300–303 (El Rastro) Pedro de Agustín, pedrodeagustin.com